TUNNELS

TUNNELS

Sam and Beryl Epstein

Little, Brown & Company
Boston   Toronto

First Edition

The following drawings and photographs appear at the beginning of each chapter: (page 2)
photograph of the Paris sewer system by Sam Epstein; (page 16) photograph of the Standedge
Canal Tunnel entrance by Sam Epstein; (page 28) photograph of the New Cascade Tunnel
courtesy Burlington Northern Railroad; (page 54) photograph of the Holland Tunnel courtesy
Port Authority of New York and New Jersey; (page 78) photograph by Sam Epstein of drawing
of the London subway construction courtesy London Transport; (page 92) drawing by Mike
Eagle based on an illustration from *The Story of the Famous Tunnel Escape from the Libby
Prison* courtesy U.S. Army Military Institute.

Library of Congress Cataloging in Publication Data

Epstein, Sam, 1909–
    Tunnels.

    Includes index.
    Summary: Describes the techniques and obstacles
involved in digging and building tunnels, from early
quanaats to the thirty-mile Seikan Tunnel in Japan.
    1. Tunnels — Juvenile literature.   2. Tunneling —
Juvenile literature.   [1. Tunnels.   2. Tunneling]
I. Epstein, Beryl Williams, 1910–   . II. Title.
TA807.E67   1985   624.1′93   85-9735
ISBN 0-316-24573-9
                            BP

Published simultaneously in Canada
by Little, Brown & Company (Canada) Limited

Printed in the United States of America

Contents

Foreword

People have been building tunnels for thousands of years and are still building them today — tunnels through mountains, across deserts, and beneath rivers, tunnels under tall city buildings and crowded city streets, secret tunnels to provide escape from walled prisons.

The building of each different kind of tunnel demands the solution to difficult problems. How can a hole be blasted through solid rock? How can a tunnel be built through soft, shifting sand or oozing mud? What special technique must be used to create a tunnel just below a traffic-laden thoroughfare? How does a desperate prisoner of war, lacking all proper digging tools, tunnel his way to freedom?

Answers to these questions, and more, are part of the fascinating stories about tunnelers and what they do. Their job has often been called one of the most difficult and most dangerous in all the world.

Thousands of tunnelers have lost their lives underground, through fire, flood, or cave-in. When the Hoosac Tunnel was being built in Massachusetts, for example, in the mid-nineteenth century, a fire broke out in a supply building constructed over a shaft leading down to the tunnel itself. Within minutes the entire flaming structure collapsed downward into the shaft. All the workmen trapped at the shaft's bottom were killed.

But catastrophes are only part of the history of tunneling. Vision is a part of it too. When most engineers were convinced that a tunnel could never be built through the towering rock masses of the Alps, the King of Sardinia decided to prove them wrong. He didn't live to see his dream become a reality, but his son carried on the father's ambitious project. And under the direction of the brilliant engineer Germaine Sommeiller, the Mount Fréjus Tunnel — first of today's many Alpine tunnels — was finally completed.

And it was a man named Marc Brunel, after studying the small destructive creature called the shipworm, who first visualized a means for burrowing through soft substances such as mud or sand. The "shield" he invented both protected his workers and made it possible for them to tunnel through the bed of silt lying under the

Thames River where it ran through London. When Brunel's labors left him unfit for work, it was again a son, Isambard, who carried it on. The Brunels' Thames Tunnel, opened in 1842, was the first tunnel ever built under water, but it was followed by the many subaqueous tunnels now in use all over the world.

Today's tunnels are built for the same purposes tunnels have always served. Among the most important of them are transporting people and goods, carrying to cities the fresh water on which they depend, and carrying away sewage. Without today's tunnels, the world as we know it could not exist.

Each tunnel has its own story. And the stories in this book are just a few of the dramatic tales that make up the long history of tunnelers and the tunnels they have built.

Acknowledgments

For their help in providing research material and illustrations, the authors thank Bethlehem Steel Corporation; British Department of Environment; British Information Service; British Railways Board; British Waterways Board; Burlington Northern Railroad; Commonwealth of Massachusetts State Library; French National Railroads; Hoosac Tunnel Museum, North Adams, Massachusetts; Hughes Tool Company; Ingersoll-Rand Company; Instituto Italiano di Cultura, New York; Japanese National Railways; Lebanon (Penn.) Public Library; London Transport; London Transport Museum; Museé Degouts de Paris; New York City Department of Environmental Protection; New York Public Library; Port Authority of New York; Riverhead (N.Y.) Free Library; Smithsonian Institution, Washington, D.C.; Southold (N.Y.) Free Library; Swiss National Tourist Office; U.S. Army Military History Institute, Carlisle, Pennsylvania.

TUNNELS

1.
Carrying Water:
Aqueducts, Qanaats, and Sewers

Our first story is about a tunnel built more than two thousand years ago. It was built — and still exists — on the little island of Samos, which lies in the Aegean Sea between Greece and what is now Turkey. As part of an aqueduct connecting a spring with the island's one city, also called Samos, it brought Samos what no other city then possessed: an abundant supply of fresh water delivered to all its inhabitants.

Two men were responsible for that tunnel. One was Polycrates, known as the Tyrant of Samos. The other was Eupalinus, the engineer who superintended its construction.

Polycrates and his two brothers had seized control of Samos not long before, in 535 B.C. Immediately after their victory, however, Polycrates had sent one brother into exile and had the other killed, leaving himself the island's sole ruler.

He found Samos a pleasant enough place. It had a fine climate and good soil. Settled some centuries earlier by the Greeks called Ionians, it had become fairly prosperous. The city of Samos hugged a hillside rising from the water's edge. Its wharves were busy. Its streets were crowded with well-built houses and shops. But in all these respects it was much like other Aegean islands. And Polycrates was determined to transform it into the most important place in the whole Greek world — the wealthiest, the most powerful, the most advanced.

His first move was to build a hundred great red-sailed ships, and send them out to raid and plunder his neighbors. The ships returned with rich cargoes of looted treasure, and with hundreds of captured prisoners who would be used as slaves. Polycrates was then ready to begin the three vast building projects that would bring fame to Samos and to himself.

One of those projects was the largest Greek temple ever built.

Another was a great stone breakwater, stretching a full quarter

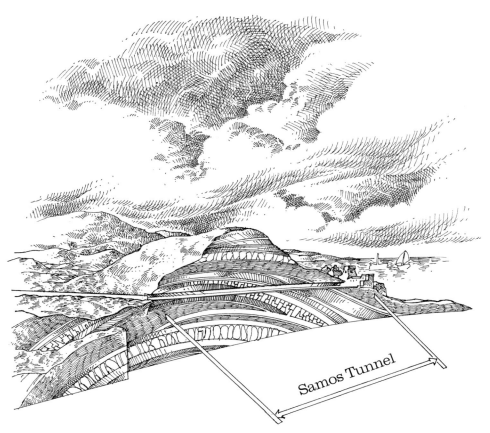

The Samos tunnel, built by Eupalinus to carry water into the sixth century B.C. city, ran through solid limestone for more than half a mile.

of a mile out to sea, into water over a hundred feet deep. The tyrant's whole fleet could ride at safe anchor in the harbor it created.

The third was the aqueduct of which the tunnel of our story formed a part — the famous tunnel of Samos.

Eupalinus had come to Samos from the Greek city of Megara. He was one of the many outstanding artists, craftsmen, and other trained professionals who had been lured to the island by the high wages Polycrates offered them. Eupalinus was not a military engineer, such as had long served rulers by building their forts and machines of war. He was what we now call a civil engineer, a builder of structures for civilian use. He is the first civil engineer whose name has come down to us.

The aqueduct he had been hired to build would begin at a spring some distance inland, beyond the hill against which the city of Samos was built. For most of its way between spring and city, it would consist simply of a clay pipe lying in a downward-slanting trough. But since that trough couldn't be carried up over the hill behind the city — even the best engineers in those days couldn't make water run uphill — the trough would have to go through the base of the hill instead. And that would require a tunnel more than half a mile long, cut through solid limestone.

Eupalinus left no report of his work, so we can't know just how he went about it. Probably he based his plans on what was then known about water-carrying tunnels.

Qanaats and the Tunnel
of King Hezekiah

Eupalinus almost certainly knew, for example, about the small tunnels with the curious name of qanaats. They had been used for centuries and are still used today in desert regions. There, precious water quickly evaporates if it is exposed to the hot sun. But it can be carried from a spring to distant fields and villages if it is sent through an underground channel. And a qanaat can carry a useful amount of water even though it is quite small. A qanaat, in fact, is generally so small that only one man — and he must be very skilled — can dig at one section of it.

A qanaat is dug in short sections, each beginning at the base of a well-like shaft driven down from the surface. This method has two advantages. First, the shaft locations — they are usually about fifty yards apart — are marked out before the work begins, and keep the tunnel along its planned route. Second, digging can begin in both directions, from the bottom of each shaft, and this means that many diggers can work on the tunnel at one time.

The soil removed from the shafts and the tunnel is piled around each shaft opening. To this day, a row of earth mounds on the desert clearly marks the route of a qanaat below.

Eupalinus may also have known of a tunnel built more than two hundred years earlier at the command of Hezekiah, King of Judah. This tunnel, less than a third of a mile long, and about six feet high, can still be seen today. It connected a spring outside Jerusalem with a reservoir inside the city's walls. There are several curves in it — and two shafts along its length.

Modern experts believe, however, that those shafts were both dug upward from the tunnel, rather than downward as is the case with a qanaat's shaft. They were dug, these experts think, because the two teams of tunnelers, one working from each end, had become "lost" in their efforts to join their two sections underground. But when each team dug a shaft up to the surface, to show its location, they could change their courses so that they could meet — so that the tunnel could be "holed through," as tunnelers say.

A description in ancient Hebrew, carved over the entrance to King Hezekiah's tunnel, describes that joining. After each team had heard the voices of the other, it says, through the cracked rock that still separated them, "the workmen struck each to meet his neighbor, pick against pick" — and they were through!

Building the Samos Tunnel

Like the Jerusalem tunnel builder, Eupalinus set to work with two crews, one working from each side of the hill at the city's back. He used no shafts. He must have believed he could keep his tunnel on course without them.

Polycrates undoubtedly supplied him with as many slave workmen as he could use. But Eupalinus may have had to teach those slaves how to handle the picks, hammers, and chisels they would work with. Probably he also had to teach them the two methods then known for breaking up stone by the use of wood.

One way was to drive a wooden wedge into a natural crack in the rock. The wedge was then kept wet with water so that the wood swelled and eventually put enough pressure on the rock to split it into pieces.

If there were no cracks in the rock, the workmen had to drill their own holes with a device called a bow drill. The bow itself was very much like one used for shooting arrows. The drill was a metal rod, probably of bronze. One end of it, dipped in emery or some other grinding powder, was pressed firmly against the rock. A wooden block, pressed against the rod's other end, held it in place. Then the bowstring was wrapped several times around the rod, so that the rod was spun first one way, then the other, when the bow was moved back and forth. The spinning rod, and the grinding powder beneath it, slowly wore a hole in the rock. And the wooden peg driven into that hole was kept wet until the rock cracked and split.

The other method of breaking up rock, called fire-setting, was to burn wood close against the rock until the rock grew hot, and then to throw water on it to produce steam. The steam could cause the rock to crack, so that it could be broken up with picks and hammers. Fire-setting, of course, added the danger of burns and suffocation to the common tunneling dangers of bad air and falling or flying rock. No one knows how many slaves were injured or killed while the Samos tunnel was being built.

Eupalinus had designed the tunnel to be about eight feet high, with an arched roof, and about eight feet wide. But all along one side of it the floor was to be dug out to form the channel, or trough, in which the clay water pipe would lie. Inspectors could walk along the floor of the tunnel, beside the channel, to check for leaks in the pipe. At the end of the tunnel nearest the spring, the channel was about eight feet deep. But it grew steadily deeper as it neared the city, to make certain that gravity would carry the water steadily downward. It was nearly thirty feet deep at the city end.

Eupalinus's crews worked on steadily for years, driving into the hill's base from opposite sides. They were nearing what they knew must be the midpoint of the hill when Eupalinus realized that

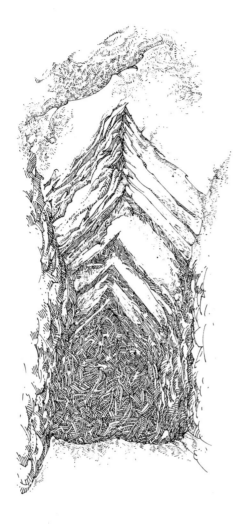

The peak-roofed entrance to the Samos tunnel can still be seen today.

their two tunnels would never meet. They were following courses that, if continued, would take them past each other with some sixteen feet of rock between them.

It's not known how he discovered the error. We do know what he did about it. He ordered one group of workmen to turn its tunnel to the right, and to continue in that direction until it ran into the other section.

At the end of fifteen years the Samos tunnel — with the two turns required to bring its halves together — was finally holed through. It remained useful long after Eupalinus died, and after Polycrates met his death at the hand of one of his many enemies. For centuries the tyrant's tunnel, along with his great temple and his harbor-forming breakwater, were known as the "three greatest works in any Greek land."

Eventually the tunnel fell into disuse because Samos dwindled into an unimportant village. But curious visitors can still walk through the peak-roofed entrance at its city end and explore most of this historic engineering feat. It had given Samos a water-supply system that was almost certainly the best of its time. It delivered water to a network of pipes that carried it directly to the city's houses, shops, public buildings, and fountains. Other pipes carried the city's waste water out to sea.

Greek and Roman Aqueducts

Polycrates and Eupalinus had in fact set an example that other cities were quick to follow. All through the Greek world the idea spread that a city could prosper and grow only if it had a dependable supply of fresh water. And since few cities could find such a supply within their own walls, more and more of them began to pipe in water from outside sources, building tunnels for their aqueducts whenever necessary.

That Greek idea was inherited by the Romans, who followed the Greeks as masters of the Mediterranean region. By the year A.D. 97, Rome's water commissioner was proud of the nine aqueducts already bringing water into the city from distant springs, lakes, and rivers. When another two had been built, the total length of Rome's aqueducts was about 260 miles, most of them underground. So it's not surprising that the Roman's Latin language gave us our word *aqueduct*. It comes from their words for *water* and for *to conduct* or *to lead*.

As Rome's empire spread through northern Africa and Europe, the Romans were never satisfied with simply building and fortifying their new towns. They also used the taxes they collected to provide each town with a water supply. Dozens of the aqueducts they built, some of them still in use, can be seen today in what are now Spain, France, and England.

The Aqua Claudia was built in A.D. 38 to bring water into Rome. It is one of the finest of Roman aqueducts.

The many sightseers who go to look at ancient Roman aqueducts do not very often see a tunnel. What they do see is a handsome bridge-like structure, made of stone or brick, perhaps covered with cement. It stretches across a valley, from one hillside to another, and supports a roofed water trough. One very famous aqueduct, known as the Pont du Gard, crosses the Gardon River valley in France.

The Pont du Gard consists of three rows of graceful stone arches,

The Pont du Gard crosses the Gardon River Valley in France. Water traveled through a trough along the top of the structure.

one built on top of the other, rising to a height of 160 feet above the river. Its cut stones fit so perfectly that they have remained in place to this day, without any mortar to hold them together. But many people who come to admire it do not realize that it exists only to join the tunnels dug centuries ago through those hills at either end of it.

The building of Roman aqueducts ended with the collapse of the Roman Empire in the fifth century A.D. The tribes of Visigoths who swept through Europe then destroyed much of what the Romans had built. And for the next several centuries Europeans lived through one war after another, suffering constantly from hunger and disease.

The missionaries who eventually appeared among the Visigoths, with the purpose of preaching Christianity, also built abbeys, which served as the first schools most people had ever seen. And those same monks and friars introduced people to an ordered way of life that had been largely forgotten.

One sign of that order, at many abbeys, was the system of pipes and channels that brought in supplies of good water. Some abbeys shared their water with a neighboring village that had been using water from polluted wells or streams. When that happened, the health of the villagers naturally improved. And later, when the abbeys fell on hard times, some of those villages became responsible for their own water supply. They were taking the first step toward today's great municipal water-supply systems.

Water for Big Cities

Every big modern city depends on such a system. Similar systems are also necessary today to produce the lush crops that now grow in areas once too dry for any kind of farming. All those modern systems have much in common with the one Eupalinus built on the island of Samos. It's true they seldom need bridge-like structures such as the Pont du Gard. Now, by means of powerful machinery, water can be pumped up and over hills. But most of today's water systems still make use of tunnels. There are 92 miles of tunnels, for example, in the 672-mile length of the Colorado River Aqueduct, one of the several vast water systems in the American West.

Many tunnels also help supply the city of New York with over a billion gallons of water a day. That water reaches the city through three separate networks, each one depending on streams and rivers draining a hilly region north of the city. Those streams and rivers are dammed to form reservoirs from which aqueducts carry the

A water supply tunnel twenty-four feet in diameter being built for New York City. *Photograph courtesy New York City Department of Environmental Protection.*

water southward to the city. There it is distributed through four local reservoirs and two huge tunnels.

One of those tunnels is eighteen miles long. The other runs for twenty miles. A third tunnel, to be finished some time in the twenty-first century, will be sixty miles long and so large that two trains could pass each other inside it. Part of it is being dug through rock six hundred feet beneath the city's skyscrapers and busy streets. It is already being called one of the engineering wonders of the world.

Like other big cities — and, once more, like Samos — New York also has a network of pipes that carry off waste water. Those pipes run through tunnels called sewers. New York City has 6,200 miles of them.

The many miles of sewers in Paris were made world-famous by the French writer Victor Hugo, who used them as the scene of a police chase in his famous novel *Les Misérables.* Today those sewers — well lighted and free of unpleasant smells — are a popular tourist attraction. In an underground museum, beneath the bank of the River Seine, visitors see photographs of earlier visitors who

A water tunnel bored by machine. *Photograph courtesy Hughes Micon, A Division of the Hughes Tool Company.*

were actually taken for leisurely boat rides through the sewers. They also see pictures and models of the machinery used to clean the miles of these huge tunnels that carry off rain and street-cleaning water from the city's streets. A slide show explains the way leaves and other debris are removed from the water before it drains into the river. And guides lead the visitors along the walkways beside a broad main sewer and several of its smaller branches.

Of course the aqueduct tunnels of today are not chipped out by slaves using picks and hammers and chisels. Today's well-paid and highly trained tunnel builders use modern machines and power tools invented in the nineteenth and twentieth centuries. Long before those inventions appeared, however, men were building the first examples of a new kind of tunnel. It had nothing to do with the aqueduct which long ago brought water to Samos, but water did flow through it — the water of a canal. Few such tunnels are still used today, but they were very important in their time. And — just as you might expect — they are called canal tunnels.

Until recently visitors could tour the sewers of Paris by boat.

Today's visitors are taken on a walking tour of parts of the Paris sewer system, such as the one above. *Photograph by Sam Epstein.*

2.
Connecting Waterways:

Canal Tunnels

Carrying people and goods from one place to another has always been necessary, and in ancient times it was done chiefly by water. Ships carried passengers and cargoes over the sea. Smaller craft followed the course of inland rivers. The artificial waterways we call canals were built where no rivers existed.

On level land a canal was nothing more than a big ditch, dug easily enough by men wielding picks and shovels. When the ditch had to cross a hill, or a valley, it was dug in level sections, each one higher than the one before — like the steps in a stairway. The sections were connected by locks: short stretches of ditch with watertight doors at both ends.

When water from the next higher section is let slowly into a lock, a boat in the lower lock rises with the water until it reaches the higher level. Then the door at the "upper" end is opened, and the boat passes through and continues on its way. By the same system, in reverse, a boat can be lowered from section to section when it is going "downhill."

The Canal Tunnels of France

In 1664 a Frenchman, the Baron Paul Riquet, made a plan for a canal that would connect two rivers in southern France. One river emptied into the Mediterranean Sea, the other into the Atlantic Ocean. The Canal du Midi, or Canal of the South, sometimes called the Languedoc Canal, would give France a continuous waterway from ocean to sea.

It was a daring project for those times. The canal would be some 150 miles long and would require more than a hundred locks. But the French government — which expected to collect tolls for its use — agreed to pay for its construction. Work began in 1666.

All went smoothly until the canal reached a hill that the Baron realized was too steep and too high to be "crossed" by a series of locks. Government engineers advised him to shift the canal's route so that it would go around the hill. The baron made the startling decision to go through the hill instead. In two years his men completed the world's first canal tunnel. Five hundred feet long, it was probably the first tunnel in which gunpowder was used to blast out rock.

The baron's birthplace, the southern French town of Béziers, honored its native son by erecting his statue on its main boulevard and giving that boulevard his name.

The French dug many other canals and canal tunnels, too, and paid for them by collecting tolls. One tunnel, in their San Quentin Canal, was three and a half miles long — a full hour's journey for the animal-hauled barges that traveled the canals. When it was officially opened, in 1810, no boatman would risk entering that long dark passage. Officials fumed at them all as cowards. Their words had no effect.

Finally the officials announced that the first boat to go through the tunnel could do so without charge, and would have free canal passage from that day on. One boatman, either braver or more greedy than the rest, immediately took advantage of that offer of a lifetime free of tolls. Into the darkness he drove his barge-pulling animals. Pale but unharmed and triumphant, he emerged from its farther end. His boat was never charged a canal fee again. And he was, of course, only the first of many boatmen who from then on used that fearsomely dark passage.

English Canal Tunnels

Canal building got a later start in England than it did in France, and most English canals were built by private companies. They too expected to profit by collecting tolls. But some English mine owners and manufacturers built their own canals for their own business purposes. The Duke of Bridgewater, for example, wanted a canal that would transport coal from his mines to the city of Manchester, some ten miles away. In 1759 he hired James Brindley to build it.

Brindley had never gone to school, but he was a genius at designing and building machinery. It was said that when he faced a particularly difficult problem, he went to bed and stayed there until he had solved it. There is no record of how long he remained in bed seeking solutions to the problems of the duke's canal, but he did find them. And the canal was built without locks, so that the coal barges could travel through it without frequent delays.

The canal began with a tunnel dug right into the mine, where the coal barges were loaded. It then crossed a valley, supported by a two-hundred-foot-long viaduct, or bridge. It ended with a tunnel into a hill at the edge of Manchester. And there the coal could be hoisted up a shaft to the surface, by means of steam-powered machinery Brindley had built. By 1761 the duke's coal was traveling from the duke's mine, on the duke's canal, to the coal-hungry factories of Manchester.

As the number of English factories increased, a network of canals to serve them was built on each side of the Pennine Chain, a range of hills that separates eastern and western England. A canal connection between the two networks was badly needed. It would require locks, and a long tunnel through one particularly high obstacle, the Standedge Ridge. In spite of the difficulties it posed, a canal company was formed to build it.

Work began in 1794. Shafts were sunk from the top of the ridge down to the level of the tunnel. Gunpowder was used to blast away at the hard rock. There were accidents — many of them — and many workmen were killed. But in 1811 the completed three-mile Standedge Tunnel was providing the first direct water route between eastern and western England.

The tunnel and the Huddersfield Narrow Canal, of which it formed a part, were closed to navigation in the early 1940s. In 1974

An entrance to the Standedge Canal Tunnel, now closed to boat traffic. *Photograph by Sam Epstein.*

canal lovers and tunnel enthusiasts formed the Huddersfield Canal Society, with the hope of restoring this historic waterway. Visitors to the area are invited to help "with your pen, your spade, your

An old drawing of two bargemen "legging" their boat through the Standedge Canal Tunnel. The three-mile journey usually took about four hours.

Bargeman David Whitehead set a record when he "legged" his barge through the Standedge Canal Tunnel in one hour and twenty-five minutes.

moral support, or in any other way you have to offer." Some stretches of the canal and its towpath have been cleared up, but the tunnel itself remains sealed.

The Standedge, like certain other English tunnels, was barely wide enough for a barge to pass through it. There was no room for the waterside path usually provided for the barge-pulling animals. Bargemen had to get their barges through such narrow tunnels by themselves. In some of these tunnels they could do it by tugging on chains fastened to the tunnel walls. In the Standedge they had to do it by "legging" — by lying on their backs, on the deck of the barge, and pushing with their feet against the tunnel's walls or roof.

American Canal Tunnels

The canal-building fever reached the United States while George Washington was still President. The first two small American canals were dug in Massachusetts, and New York's 350-mile-long Erie Canal was started in 1817. None of those three canals needed a tunnel.

So the first canal tunnel in the United States was the one dug in 1818 through a 450-foot ridge near the Pennsylvania town of Orwigsburg. And that tunnel, people said, wouldn't have been needed if the canal's course had been shifted only slightly. Apparently its builders simply wanted a tunnel in order to attract attention to their canal.

If that was so, they certainly succeeded. People came from Philadelphia by the hundreds to watch the laboring miners, as rock tunnelers have always been called.

In 1824 the second American canal tunnel was blasted through a 700-foot rock ridge near Lebanon, another Pennsylvania town. The Union Canal that went through it has, like so many other canals, been long abandoned, but the carefully preserved tunnel still attracts visitors. Often, when they arrive to peer into it, they are greeted by a nearby resident who enjoys answering their questions and gives them a picture postcard of the neatly arched opening.

The Union Canal Tunnel near Lebanon, Pennsylvania, is the oldest tunnel in the United States. It was blasted through solid rock between 1824 and 1827. *Photograph by Sam Epstein.*

How Tunnelers Work

The miners who dug canal tunnels all worked in much the same way, following a system still used for tunneling through rock. They carried out a series of operations known as "rounds."

A round starts with the drilling of holes in the tunnel face, the solid wall of rock facing the miners as they work. The holes are filled with explosives. The blasts are set off. The tunnel is cleared of the smoke and dust the explosions have left. Men called "muckers" haul away the loose rock, or muck. Then a new round begins.

A tunneler describes his round as drill, load, blast, ventilate, and remove rock. It can be described much more quickly than it can be carried out.

Drilling used to be done most commonly by what miners called

Mucking with hand-operated equipment in a mid-nineteenth-century tunnel. The muckers are standing in water, and working by the light of candles fastened to their hats. In the background miners are drilling blasting holes up near the tunnel roof. *Drawing from* Frank Leslie's Illustrated Newspaper.

"double jacking": two men, each with a sledgehammer, took turns pounding the steel drill their helper held in place. The helper's hand could be badly crushed if the sledgehammer missed its mark.

After each hammer blow the helper turned the drill slightly in its hole, to prevent its sharp end from becoming wedged tightly in the rock. And every few minutes the miners stopped long enough to allow their helper to pull out the drill, and use a sort of long-handled spoon to clean the rock dust out of the hole.

Drills became dull very quickly. "Nipper boys," as they were called, were kept busy carrying those heavy drills out of the tunnel to the blacksmith shop, for sharpening, and delivering newly sharpened ones to the drill teams.

Each drill hole was an inch or so in diameter, and three or four feet long by the time it was finished. Many holes had to be drilled for each round. Their number and location on the face depended on the hardness of the rock and the size of the face. Generally, miners drilled a group of holes in the center of the face and others, more widely spaced, around that group. Some holes went straight into the rock; others were drilled at various angles. By firing the explosives in the central holes first, a cavity was blasted out of the center of the face and the rock around it was weakened. The following explosions usually shattered the rest of the drilled area.

If the blasting holes were four feet deep, the blasts loosened about four feet of rock. Then, after the shattered rock had been cleared away, the tunnel was about four feet longer than it had been when the round started.

In some cases miners began digging the upper half of a tunnel first. When that half had been dug for a distance of eight or ten feet, and while work on it continued, other miners behind them started work on the tunnel's bottom half. This allowed more men to work in the small space at the tunnel face without getting in each other's way.

In other cases, where the rock was weak, miners sometimes dug channels on both sides of the tunnel first, leaving the middle section untouched for a time. That untouched section kept the tunnel roof from caving in until workers could begin lining it with brick or stone.

Preventing a tunnel from caving in was, and often still is, one of the most difficult parts of a tunnel job. How it is done depends

The upper part of this mid-nineteenth-century tunnel is farther advanced than the lower part. The miners on top are drilling for a new round of blasting. The muckers below are removing already blasted rock. *Drawing courtesy Ingersoll-Rand Company.*

on what tunnel men call the "stand-up time" of the material they're digging through. By this they mean the length of time that material will stand without support. Hard rock may have a stand-up time of many years, or even centuries. Layered rock may sometimes be left without support for weeks or months. But soft rock may crumble within hours, especially where water has seeped into it. And gravel, soft earth, and sand may have almost no stand-up time at all.

Early tunnel men didn't have much trouble when the stand-up time was as long as several days or weeks. Then the miners and muckers could move steadily ahead, while masons or carpenters worked behind them to strengthen the tunnel's walls and roof with masonry or heavy timbers. But if there was little stand-up time, the miners had to support the roof as they went along. This was slow and dangerous work.

One way to do it was to drive heavy planks into the earth a few feet ahead of them, at roof height. Those planks, supported by upright timbers, became a wooden ceiling under which the miners could go on digging. And they drove in more planks as they advanced, each time extending the protective wooden ceiling another few feet.

There were no schools where the early canal-tunnel builders could learn how to keep a tunnel from caving in, where to drill their blasting holes, or any of the many other things they had to know. Experience was their only teacher, and they passed on what they had learned to those who came after them. By the time canal building had reached its peak, tunnelers had collected a great deal of information. They were ready to start boring tunnels for the newer and faster means of transportation that began to replace canals in the mid 1800s.

3.
Blasting through Mountains:

Railroad Tunnels

In 1814 George Stephenson, a self-educated English engineer, mounted a coal-fired steam engine on a sort of wagon and called the contraption a locomotive. He had the idea that it could take the place of the horses then pulling cars along the tracks of the recently built "railway" lines. He proved it could. It pulled a train of loaded coal cars at a speed horses couldn't match.

Eleven years later a Stephenson steam-driven locomotive officially replaced the horses on England's Stockton & Darlington Railway. The Railway Age, as it came to be known, had begun. It would change centuries-old ways of life.

Some people objected to that. Others felt a new freedom and excitement. Now they could visit places they had never expected to see. Now farmers could send their produce quickly to markets in distant cities. Now shopkeepers could receive quick shipments of goods from the new factories springing up everywhere.

Railway engineers realized from the start that a locomotive can't pull a train up most hills, because on a steep slope its wheels just spin uselessly on the rails. So they carried their lines around the base of hills where that was possible. Or they built zigzagging tracks called switchbacks to carry trains gradually up one side of a hill and down the other. And in places where they couldn't go around a hill, or zigzag over it, the railroad engineers did what canal builders had done before them: they dug tunnels.

Steam-Railway Tunnels

A little tunnel had been dug in France around 1826 for a horse-drawn railway line. But George Stephenson was the engineer of the world's first two steam-railway tunnels. Both were for a rail line connecting the port city of Liverpool with textile-manufacturing Manchester about forty miles away. One tunnel was over half a mile long, the other nearly a mile.

Built like canal tunnels, by the slow, back-breaking labor of men and animals, Stephenson's tunnels had their share of cave-

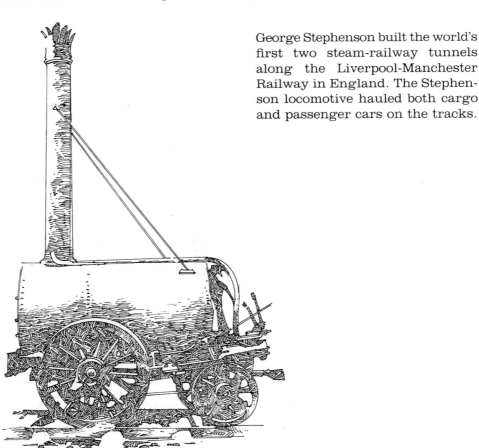

George Stephenson built the world's first two steam-railway tunnels along the Liverpool-Manchester Railway in England. The Stephenson locomotive hauled both cargo and passenger cars on the tracks.

ins, injuries, and deaths. But he got the job done in time for the Liverpool-Manchester Railway to open on September 15, 1830. And eight Stephenson locomotives were ready, by then, to pull cars along its tracks and through the two brick-lined tunnels he had engineered.

Those locomotives, belching black clouds of cinders and smoke, immediately roused concern over the safety of steam-railway tunnels. Train crews and passengers — everyone who rode through a tunnel behind one of those locomotives — had the same complaints. The thunderous noise made their ears ache; some said their hearing had been damaged. Their faces and clothes were blackened, their eyes were streaming, they were coughing and gasping for breath. Many had been terrified that they would actually die of suffocation. Doctors issued solemn warnings that steam-railway tunnels were a danger to the public's health.

Even the tunnel builders themselves admitted that riding through a tunnel behind a locomotive was unpleasant, to say the least. But they felt it was a price people should be willing to pay for the booming industrial progress of the time. So the tunnel building went on.

Joseph Locke, for example, who had learned about railroading from Stephenson, was one of the busy new tunnel engineers. He was hired to build a pair of three-mile-long tunnels through a hill in the Pennines, the range of hills already pierced by several canal tunnels. One of the pair was to carry the trains running from Manchester to steel-producing Sheffield, the other to carry trains traveling in the opposite direction. In December 1845, when Locke finished the first of those Woodhead Tunnels, as they were called, it was famous as the longest railroad tunnel in the world. But before its twin could be completed, six years later, that honor belonged to another Pennine tunnel, the new Standedge Railroad Tunnel dug right alongside the Standedge Canal Tunnel. The Standedge Railroad Tunnel was some 150 feet longer than the two Woodheads.

Railroads and railroad tunnels were being built on the European continent too, almost as fast as they were in England. Germany, France, and Belgium had such tunnels in the 1830s. Austria and Italy had them not long afterward.

The first one built in the United States, in 1835, was on the route of an unusual railroad line, the Allegheny Portage Railroad. That line had been designed to take the place of locks, where canal barges had to cross a range of low Pennsylvania hills. The barges were loaded on special railroad cars, pulled over the hills by cables, and unloaded into the canal beyond them. The railroad has long since vanished, but its single little tunnel, the 700-foot-long Staple Bend Tunnel near Johnstown, can still be seen today.

While those early railroad tunnels were being dug, advances were being made in science and engineering that would affect all future tunnel building. Geologists were acquiring new knowledge of rocks and underground water, and it would help tunnelers know what to expect before they drilled their first blast holes. Improved surveying instruments would make it possible to survey a railroad line and its tunnels more accurately than ever before. Ways were being found, by chemists and physicists, to improve the metals used for tools and machinery.

And in schools and colleges a new kind of expert was being educated: the mechanical engineer. His training prepared him for the special job of designing and building machines to do work that for centuries had been done by human and animal labor. Those new mechanical engineers would carry forward the pioneering efforts of such self-educated machine-building geniuses as Brindley and Stephenson of England, and America's Eli Whitney and Robert Fulton.

The stories of two tunnels started in the 1850s — one in the United States, the other in Europe — tell us what went on in the world of tunneling as a result of some of those changes. Each of those tunnels — they were the longest ever attempted up to that time — was started by the same methods used in earlier tunnels bored through rock. But in each tunnel, before it was finished, new machinery was operating alongside the men working deep inside a mountain.

One of those tunnels was driven through Hoosac Mountain in the Berkshire Hills of northwestern Massachusetts. The other was bored through a mountain in the mighty European range called the Alps.

The Hoosac Tunnel

A tunnel through Hoosac Mountain was first proposed because New York State was building the Erie Canal from the Hudson River to

Lake Erie. And the proposal seemed very sound to many people in Massachusetts.

A completed Erie Canal was going to give New York City, at the Hudson's mouth, a direct waterway to the Great Lakes and the growing markets of the Midwest. These were the same markets Massachusetts businessmen and manufacturers hoped to profit from. But to reach those markets they, too, needed a waterway to the Great Lakes. And the best way to obtain it, they believed, was to build a canal from Boston to the Hudson River. The logical route for such a canal would require a tunnel through Hoosac Mountain.

The Erie Canal was finished in 1825. Boston's dreamed-of canal had not yet even been started, and now the plans for it were abandoned. By 1825 railroads were beginning to replace canals, and in Massachusetts it was suggested that a rail line be built along the canal route that had already been mapped out.

Twenty years passed before plans were finally agreed upon to build and join together a group of short rail lines that would reach from Boston to the Hudson River. One of those rail lines, the Troy and Greenfield Railroad Company, accepted the responsibility for building the Hoosac Tunnel. It would be about four and three-quarters miles long.

The railroad's engineer estimated that the tunnel could be dug in 1,556 days by two sets of crews, one working from each side of the mountain. Or, he said, it could be done in only 1,054 days if there was a central shaft to allow two more sets of crews to work on it. He also estimated the cost of the tunnel, just as specifically, down to the last dollar, at $1,948,557.

As it turned out the Hoosac Tunnel job would last more than twenty years and cost about $17,000,000. Although the railroad company itself started the work, it soon turned the job over to one contractor, and later to another. When the railroad company went bankrupt in 1861, the whole project came to a halt. Then the state took over, and in 1863 it dug the still-lacking central shaft. But the state, too, eventually turned the job over to a contractor and it was he, a Canadian, who actually completed the tunnel in 1873.

The details of all those changes in management now fill volumes in the State Archives in Boston. Those archives also contain details of just how the actual tunneling was done.

Work on the tunnel began in 1851 on the west side of the mountain. A year later work began on the east side. And that day a small crowd of state and railroad officials gathered there to see a new tunneling machine for which the railroad company had paid $25,000. Powered by a steam engine, it was rather like a monstrous cookie cutter. It had been designed to cut a neat twenty-four-foot circle in the mountain's stone face.

The machine's boiler was fired up. Smoke belched from its stack. Then, to the sound of hissing steam, stone chips began flying from its cutting teeth as they ate away at the rock. The machine chewed four inches into Hoosac's side before the excited onlookers left. Railroad officials bragged that the new machine would cut the length of the tunneling job to a brief two years.

But several days later, when the machine had dug about ten feet into the mountain, its main shaft snapped and it stopped. It would never work again. A successful machine of its kind could not be built until better metals and more advanced mechanical skills were developed.

A picture of the "cookie cutter" tunnel-boring machine that began work at the west portal of the Hoosac Tunnel. After cutting ten feet into the mountain, it broke down and had to be abandoned. *Courtesy Massachusetts State Library.*

So the miners went back to their old method of drilling, blasting, and mucking. On the east side of the mountain they made good progress. The engineer reported that digging out the hard stone there was "as straightforward and really comfortable a piece of underground work as could be wished for."

No engineer ever said anything like that about work at the tunnel's west portal. There the rock was limestone, easy to shatter but with water pouring out of every crack in it. Beneath the limestone was a muddy gravel the miners called "demoralized rock." They said handling it was like trying to shovel up a pile of wriggling eels. Steam-powered pumps therefore had to be installed at that end, to drain the water away, and every foot of the excavation had to be lined. The timbers first used as a lining collapsed so fast, under the weight of the shifting rock, that they had to be replaced by half a dozen layers of brick. Under such circumstances progress was extremely slow.

The thousand or so workers on the Hoosac Tunnel lived in village-sized camps, one on each side of the mountain. Each camp had its blacksmith and machine shops, its supply storehouses and engineers' offices. There were hastily built shacks for men with families, and shoddy boardinghouses for single men. There was a store, a saloon, and a dance hall — but no hospital and no school. Neither railroad nor government officials thought it was necessary

The west portal of the Hoosac Tunnel during construction. The women standing on top of the scaffolding had come to watch the tunnel work. *Photograph courtesy Massachusetts State Library.*

to provide decent living conditions for the miners, or for their wives and children.

When the railroad's bankruptcy brought the entire project to a halt, after ten years, only one-fifth of the tunnel had been dug. Before the state took it over, the following year, an engineer was sent to Europe to study the tunneling methods being used there. He visited what was then one of the world's most famous engineering ventures: the tunnel being dug through Mount Fréjus in the southern Alps. He realized that the new devices and techniques he saw there could and should be used on the Hoosac.

He saw, for example, mechanical drills that could punch holes in the Alpine rock at a rate far faster than the most expert hammer-swinging miner could achieve. Like the jackhammers used today, to rip up city pavements, they were powered by releasing air that had been compressed or "squeezed" into tanks. He saw the machines that compressed the air, and the dams that provided water power for those air compressors.

As soon as he returned to Massachusetts he put his knowledge to use. Work on the tunnel began to go more rapidly than it ever had before. Air drills were being used by the crews at both portals, by those digging in both directions from a shaft newly sunk through the western flank of the mountain, and by the miners finally at work on a huge central shaft. That oval-shaped shaft would have to go down a thousand feet to reach the level of the tunnel floor.

Not long afterward new and better compressed-air drills were put to work. Invented in Philadelphia, they were lighter to handle and could drill larger holes than those copied from the European designs. And Hoosac miners also began to pack their blast holes with a new explosive called nitroglycerine. It was a thick, yellowish, oily liquid, dangerous to use, but with ten times the explosive power of gunpowder. From then on their blast holes were made deeper, and a single blast might loosen as much as eight feet of rock — twice the amount of a gunpowder blast. And when electricity was introduced, to fire the nitroglycerine charges, a drill boss could set a whole group of them off at once, or one by one in whatever order was necessary for the best result.

The accidental explosion of nitroglycerine inside the tunnel was always possible, and great care was taken to avoid such a disaster. But the most terrible disaster that did occur during the digging of the Hoosac had nothing to do with that dangerous explosive.

On October 19, 1867, a fire broke out in the large building that had been erected over the slowly deepening central shaft. In that building were tons of supplies and equipment, a machine shop, a blacksmith shop, and the steam engine by which men and materials were hoisted up and down the shaft. As the flames crackled and roared through the flimsy structure, miners and their wives and children watched in horror. Then suddenly the flaming building,

The entrance to the central shaft of the Hoosac Tunnel. In 1867 the structure at the top of the shaft collapsed into it in flames. The thirteen men trapped below it were killed.

and all it contained, crashed downward into the shaft. Thirteen men had been trapped there when the fire started. None of them survived.

The public blamed the state for having failed to prevent such a catastrophe. Some people said the state should abandon the "bloody pit," or at least place the job in the more competent hands of a private contractor. The Massachusetts legislature responded by hiring the Canadian company that would finally complete the Hoosac.

The new management speeded up the work by importing another new piece of equipment then being used on the Fréjus Tunnel. It was a drilling machine, on a wheeled carriage, that could drill as many as eight holes at once. And after the completion of the central shaft, tunneling was begun in both directions from its floor. Miners were now working at six faces at once.

The Canadians also improved the conditions in the work camps, and showed a concern for the camp-dwellers' welfare that was unusual for that time. Better houses, a school, and a meeting house were built in each camp. The medical expenses of injured workers were paid, and support was given to the families of those who had died on the job.

Of course there continued to be accidents inside the tunnel. Once a hundred workers barely escaped drowning when heavy rains caused a brook to overflow right through the west portal, filling that part of the tunnel almost to its roof. Other workers were less fortunate. Before the Hoosac was finished, a great number of them had been injured, and at least two hundred men had lost their lives.

On December 12, 1872, crews working from the east portal met those working toward them from the central shaft. Half the tunnel was finished. The other half was completed less than a year later, on Thanksgiving Day, 1873. When the final holing-through occurred, there was a great celebration. The various sections had met almost perfectly, within half an inch of each other.

Another two years went by while more than twenty million bricks were used to line the walls and ceiling where they seemed likely to crumble, and while two pairs of tracks were laid, and drainage pipes were installed. The inaugural ride through the four-and-three-quarter-mile tunnel took place on February 19, 1875.

It lasted thirty-four minutes. The dignitaries riding through the darkness, in the three open cars behind the locomotive, were covered with soot at the end of it, and nearly choking. So were the locomotive engineer and fireman in their cab, although they had wrapped wet cloths around their heads and crouched low on the floor.

Even after a huge ventilation fan was installed atop the central shaft in 1897, the Hoosac remained a dirty, smoky tunnel. It was improved only after it was electrified in 1911. Then, as a train approached the tunnel, the fire of its locomotive was banked, and an electric locomotive was attached to pull the train through. Diesel engines replaced steam engines on the entire railroad in 1958. They pull trains through without the need for electric locomotives.

In 1959 the line's owner, then the Boston and Main Railroad, removed one of the tunnel's two tracks and shifted the remaining one to the center. This provided enough headroom for the new tall freight cars being used to haul automobiles.

Today freight cars are the only cars that go through the Hoosac, and they do not run on a regular schedule. But a track-walker appears at the tunnel every day, to walk its full length from the east portal to the west portal and then back again. He swings a

A trackwalker coming out of the east portal of the Hoosac Tunnel after completing his daily inspection of its entire length. *Photograph by Sam Epstein.*

flashlight slowly before him as he goes, so that every foot of the track, and the tunnel's walls and ceiling, are lit up for his inspection.

The Hoosac's long story is kept very much alive today in the photographs and other exhibits in the Hoosac Tunnel Museum in North Adams, Massachusetts, a town not far from the tunnel's west portal. The museum was established in 1980 in a carefully restored railroad passenger car, set up on its own short stretch of track beside the once busy freight yard of the Boston and Main Railroad. It will have a larger and more permanent home when that yard, with its maze of unused tracks and its empty warehouses, has been developed into the Western Gateway Heritage State Park.

The Fréjus Tunnel

To the European railroad builders of the mid 1800s, the mighty Alps were not a wonder of nature, to be gazed at with admiring awe. They were simply a great obstacle preventing those builders from linking together the rail lines already in operation on both sides of those mountains.

Men on foot and horseback, and in animal-drawn vehicles, had been crossing the Alps for centuries — except during the winter — over trails that led through mountain passes. But those trails could not be used as routes for railroads because, first of all, they were far too steep. And the fifty feet or more of snow that buried them every year, and the avalanches that swept down over them, would have made year-round railroad traffic impossible in any case.

Various railroad companies did consider tunneling through the Alps, and sent out engineers to report on the possibilities. Most reports said the same thing: any tunnel through an Alpine mountain would have to be built below the snow line, so that the tracks leading to it would be safely snow-free. But tunneling below the snow line would mean boring through the lower part of a mountain, where it has broadened out into a rock mass of enormous size.

Digging a tunnel through such a mass, engineers believed, would be impossible. For one thing, they said, the necessary ventilation shafts could not be dug down to the tunnel level from heights thousands of feet above it. For another thing, the temperature at tunnel level, so far below the surface, was likely to be too high for human beings to endure.

But one man, Carlo Alberto, King of Sardinia, was ignoring such reports. His kingdom included part of the Alpine region in what is now northern Italy and southeastern France. And he wanted his small country to prove that it could do what so many experts said could not be done: bore a tunnel through the Alps. Such a tunnel would make it possible to connect the railroads of Sardinia with those of France.

By 1845 Carlo Alberto had geologists, engineers, and surveyors planning the tunnel and the route of the railroad to it. The placement of the tunnel had been suggested by a man who had herded sheep in Alpine pastures as a boy, and who knew more than most engineers about that part of the world.

The rail line was planned to go northward from the now-Italian city of Turin, along a gently rising valley, to the tiny village of Bardonecchia clinging to the rocky side of Mount Fréjus. There, at about 3,400 feet above sea level, the tracks would go through the mountain by means of a tunnel that would have to be seven and a half miles long. From the village of Fourneaux, on the far side of Mount Fréjus, the railroad would descend along the river valleys to connect with the French railroad.

In 1849, shortly before Carlo Alberto's death, his son Victor Emmanuel II took the throne. By then much of the railroad work was accomplished. But not even the surveys for its tunnel were completed, because they had been so frequently interrupted by severe winter weather. They continued without pause under Sardinia's new king, who was as determined as his father to complete the first trans-Alp rail line.

The engineer then in charge of that line was thirty-four-year-old Germaine Sommeiller. He had already supervised the building of the railroad from Turin to Bardonecchia. And while the tunnel survey was being finished, he planned the tunnel's actual construction and the workers' villages he would build at each end of it.

He also redesigned the rock drill miners were then using, so that it was powered by compressed air rather than steam. To supply that kind of power he designed air compressors, and dams to create the water power that would run them. He expected to ventilate the

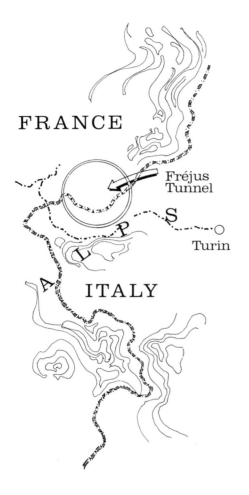

FRANCE

Fréjus
Tunnel

A L P S

Turin

ITALY

The region of northern Italy and southeastern France where King Carlo Alberto of Sardinia planned to build the first Alpine tunnel.

tunnel by the quantities of fresh air his air-powered drills would give off. These drills were among the things that so impressed the Hoosac Tunnel engineer during his visit to Europe.

In 1857, before all the carefully planned new equipment had been installed, the first rounds of blasts were set off, one on each side of Mount Fréjus. Until the machinery was at hand, the crews had to use hand drills and gunpowder, and they dug out only ten inches of rock each twenty-four-hour workday. Later, using their new air drills, their daily progress was eighteen inches. By 1864, with the same lighter and faster American-designed drills then being used at Hoosac, their rate rose dramatically to more than nine feet a day. And when the eight-drill carriages were put to work, the speed of digging increased to over fourteen feet every twenty-four hours.

The Fréjus crews were well cared for in their new towns. Single men lived in comfortable dormitories. Men with families occupied small apartments. Each town had its hospital, school, clubhouse, and recreation area.

Conditions inside the tunnel were also better than many miners had expected. The temperature there never rose as high as engineers had warned it might. Thousands of feet beneath the mountain's peak the stone did feel warm to the touch, but it never grew dangerously hot. And when problems arose they were solved. The

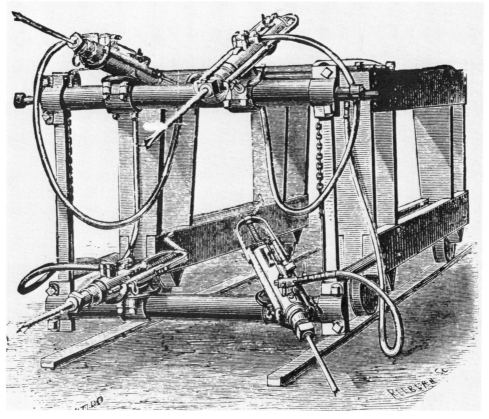

The kind of drill carriage used in the Fréjus and Hoosac tunnels. *Drawing courtesy Ingersoll-Rand Company.*

new rapid drilling, for example, resulted in choking clouds of rock dust; but water nozzles attached to the drills turned the dust into mud, and the mud was washed away by the tunnel's drainage system.

Another problem required a more elaborate solution. The good air provided to miners using the air drills didn't reach the muckers and masons working behind them. A temporary ceiling was therefore built, halfway between the tunnel's floor and its roof, to divide the whole excavation into upper and lower levels. Then powerful water-power-driven fans were installed, to force fresh air into the lower section. That air, forced toward the face, rose there into the upper section and was then forced back to the portal and out of the tunnel. By this constant circulation, every part of the tunnel was provided with good air.

It is not surprising that work on the Fréjus Tunnel went forward as steadily as it did. It was, after all, supported by a wealthy king and engineered by the skillful Sommeiller. Even Sardinia's costly war with Austria didn't halt its progress, although when that war was over Sardinia was no longer the tunnel's sole owner. France had aided Victor Emmanuel II in his struggle with Austria, and in return he had ceded to his ally some of his territory, including the north slope of Mount Fréjus. From then on the Fréjus Tunnel was an international project, and France paid half its cost.

On the day after Christmas, in the year 1870, the last blast of the Fréjus was fired. Miners from both sides rushed toward each other with shouts of victory over their holing-through. They had built the first tunnel through the Alps and the longest tunnel in the world.

The official opening of the Fréjus Tunnel — sometimes called the Mont Cenis Tunnel, from the name of a nearby mountain pass — took place on September 17, 1871. Many of the most important people of Europe were there, eager to be among the first to travel from Italy to France by way of a tunnel through the Alps.

Sommellier was not present that day. He had died several months before — from overwork, people said. But he was highly honored for having achieved the most daring piece of tunneling ever undertaken up to that time. He was also honored, as he still is, for the constant concern he showed for the health and safety of his crews. Compared to the casualty figures for the Hoosac Tunnel, those for the Fréjus were remarkably low: only fifty-four men had suffered injuries, and only twenty-eight of those had died.

Boring More Tunnels through the Alps

Even before the Fréjus was open, plans were being made for other tunnels through the Alps.

In 1872 work began on the St. Gotthard Tunnel in Switzerland. It's completion after ten years was marked by a great celebration. But for each of those years some twenty-five men had died and hundreds had been injured. Hundreds more were made lifelong invalids by the unsanitary living conditions and by an infectious disease that swept through the camps.

The Arlberg Tunnel in Austria had a happier story. Improved machinery, good working conditions, and the absence of unexpected problems made it one of the "easier" European tunnels. Begun in 1880, it was finished in 1884, more than a year ahead of schedule.

By the end of the nineteenth century Europe's experienced engineers were ready to undertake the most ambitious tunnel yet attempted: a hole twelve miles long through Mount Leone. The tracks

Celebrating the holing-through of the St. Gotthard Tunnel, February 29, 1880. *Drawing courtesy Swiss National Tourist Office.*

The first train through the St. Gotthard Tunnel on its arrival in Italy from Switzerland, June 1, 1882. *Drawing courtesy Swiss National Tourist Office.*

running through it would connect the rail lines of Italy and Switzerland, and both nations would have a hand in building it. Called the Simplon Tunnel, after a mountain pass through which Napoleon had built a road a century earlier, it would be dug at about two thousand feet above sea level — seven thousand feet below Mount Leone's peak.

Eventually it was going to be a double tunnel — Simplon One and Simplon Two — providing train traffic in both directions at the same time. Only Simplon One, however, was to be enlarged to full size immediately. During its construction the smaller Simplon Two, connected to it by cross-tunnels, would help ventilate and drain it, and serve as its supply route. Work began in 1898 on both tunnels from both sides of the mountain.

Geologists had reported that the rock of Mount Leone would present no serious difficulties. Bright electric lights were taking the place of earlier tunnelers' smoky oil lamps. Locomotives running on clean compressed air were replacing the animals previously used. Laundries supplied the workers with clean work clothes at the start of each shift, and bathhouses gave them the chance to clean up at its end. But in spite of such improvements, and that cheerful geological forecast, the Simplon was plagued with trouble from the start.

Danger threatened the whole crew near the southern portal, for example, when scalding water erupted out of the rock there while icy water was pouring from the tunnel roof nearby. In some areas the heat was so intense that cold water had to be sprayed into the ventilating pipes to keep those parts of the tunnel cool enough to work in. And there was one section where the rock turned into soft clay as soon as it was exposed to air and moisture. Even oak timbers were not enough to keep that clay from collapsing. The miners had to erect a series of steel frames into a kind of narrow corridor 140 feet long. Then, protected by those frames, they surrounded the corridor with thick masonry walls, roof, and floor. That structure alone cost them six months of time.

Nevertheless Simplon One was finished in less than seven years. On January 25, 1906, an electric locomotive pulled the first train through what was then by far the longest tunnel in the world — some four miles longer than the once-record-holding Fréjus. Even when Simplon Two was enlarged and went into operation, in 1922, no longer tunnel had yet been built anywhere. In fact the twelve-mile Simplon remained the world's longest train tunnel for more than seventy years. It lost that title only when the Dai-Shimuzu Tunnel was holed through Japan's Tanigawa Mountain in 1979. The Dai-Shimuzu is thirteen miles long.

An American Railroad Tunnel

The United States has its share of mighty mountains, too, and for early railroad builders they were as troublesome as the Alps. The Great Northern Railway, for example, faced the obstacle of the Cascade range on its route from Minneapolis to Seattle.

That line was first carried up to and through mountain passes by zigzagging switchbacks. Miles of its tracks were roofed over by snowsheds, as they are called, to keep them clear in winter. But when huge snowdrifts piled up on unprotected stretches of track, powerful snowplows had to be brought in to make them passable.

One troublesome portion of that line was replaced by the two-and-a-half-mile Cascade Tunnel in 1900. Twenty-five years later work was started on another tunnel, which was to replace it and eliminate more than seven additional miles of snowshedded track. The New Cascade Tunnel, dug lower on the mountain than the first one, was to be nearly eight miles long.

Like Simplon One, the New Cascade was dug together with a small parallel tunnel, and it too ran into underground water and

Mucking in the west portal of the New Cascade Tunnel. *Photograph courtesy Burlington Northern Railroad.*

other problems. But its engineers had the help of new and improved machinery. Its drilling rig could drill twenty-eight eight-foot-deep holes in an hour and a half. Its air-powered loading machines scooped up the blasted rock and dumped it into the small railroad cars that carried it away. And smoke from the blasting was cleared in less than half an hour by powerful ventilating fans. An average round could thus be completed in five hours, and the digging speed reached a rate of forty feet in a twenty-four-hour day.

The New Cascade was opened in 1929. It was the longest railroad tunnel in the United States. It still is.

Modern Rock-Tunnel Building

Since 1929, of course, tunneling machinery has been even further improved.

Drilling in a large tunnel today is usually done from a jumbo, a wheeled platform almost as wide and high as the tunnel itself. A jumbo may carry more than twenty miners and their hammering drills on its several platforms or "decks," as tunnelers call them. On such a machine miners can drill the top, the middle, and the bottom of a tunnel at the same time.

Rock-loading machines working beneath a jumbo can now remove the broken rock from one blasting round while the miners drill holes for the next. The rock may then be carried away by huge diesel trucks that drive right up to the face. Or the blasted rock and earth may be mixed with water and pumped out of the tunnel through large pipes.

Today there are also new methods to prevent the splitting and collapse of soft rock. One way is to cement into it the long steel rods called rock bolts. Another method, called "shotcreting," uses a high-pressure air gun, something like a paint sprayer, to spray the rock itself with a mixture of cement and water. Several inches of this mixture can be sprayed on at once, and other layers can be added after the first has hardened. Some tunnels today are permanently lined with six inches or more of this sprayed-on concrete.

The machine called a "mechanical mole" is probably the twentieth century's most important contribution to tunneling through soft rock, limestone, or shale. Not all moles are alike, but they all

Drill jumbo used in boring the Mont Blanc vehicular tunnel through the highest mountain in the European Alps. It weighs over seventy tons. *Photograph courtesy Ingersoll-Rand Company.*

work in pretty much the same way, and have descended from that unsuccessful "cookie cutter" tried out at the Hoosac Tunnel.

The front end of a mole, equipped with sharp steel-cutting wheels, revolves slowly as it is forced against the tunnel face by powerful jacks. The cutting wheels also revolve and chew away at the rock. The rock bits fall onto a broad moving belt or conveyor, which carries them to the truck that hauls them out of the tunnel.

The diameter of a mole is as large as the tunnel it is digging, and some are very large indeed. One, built to bore a water tunnel at a power dam in Pakistan, measures thirty-seven feet across. Whatever its size, it works with great speed, compared to the forty-foot-a-day progress that seemed so remarkable on the New Cascade Tunnel. A mechanical mole can dig a full-size tunnel at a rate of over three hundred feet a day. So even though it may cost several million dollars, it can prove to be a profitable investment.

These are only a few of the modern improvements in land tunneling. Others are constantly being sought. Better steels will prob-

This boring machine can cut a twenty-foot-diameter hole through rock. *Photograph courtesy Hughes Micon, A Division of the Hughes Tool Company.*

ably still further increase the speed of mechanical moles, and moles may some day be run by engineers using remote controls from a tunnel portal. In that case a mole may replace miners entirely, and dig, muck, and line a tunnel all by itself.

Experiments also go on to find chemical means for hardening rock that is too soft, and softening rock that is unmanageably hard. And engineers are experimenting with high-pressure water jets, hot jets of flame, and laser beams. Perhaps one or more of those methods will some day replace even that modern wonder, the mechanical mole.

Not many railroad tunnels are being dug today, because few new railroads are being built. But the building of another kind of transportation tunnel — a tunnel to carry cars, buses, and trucks — does go on. Some of these vehicular tunnels, as they are called, have

Interior of Mont Blanc vehicular tunnel. *Photograph courtesy Italian Cultural Institute.*

been built alongside such historic railroad tunnels as the Fréjus and the Simplon. Those vehicular tunnels are land tunnels, of course, but others have been dug beneath rivers or bays. Called underwater, or subaqueous, tunnels, they require building methods very different from those used on land. But, like land tunnels, they too have a history that goes back thousands of years.

4.
Through Mud and Silt:

Underwater Tunnels

Some four thousand years ago, the story goes, the world's first underwater tunnel was built beneath the Euphrates River where that river flowed through the ancient city of Babylon. Whether that tunnel ever really existed is impossible to say, because nothing can be seen of it today. But this is the story that is told about it.

The Euphrates Tunnel
and Cut-and-Cover Tunneling

The Euphrates River divided Babylon into two halves, each surrounded by a high wall that protected its citizens from ever-threatening enemy raiders. But Babylonians who wanted to go from one half of the city to the other had to cross the unprotected river. And even the well-guarded queen declared she was afraid to leave her palace on one side of the river to worship in the temple on the other side. She therefore ordered that the city's halves be connected by a tunnel whose two ends were safely inside the walls.

According to the story, the workmen used the method now called "cut-and-cover." First they dug a new channel for the river that would carry it around the city rather than through it. Then they dammed the river and forced it into its new channel. Next they dug a big ditch across the now dry riverbed, and extended it under the wall on either side. They lined and roofed the ditch with bricks, and waterproofed the bricks with asphalt.

When they removed the temporary dam, and allowed the river to flow back into its old course, the whole new structure was completely covered by the water. And from then on the queen — and her subjects, too — could walk safely back and forth from one half of Babylon to the other.

The cut-and-cover method is often used today, especially when a subway tunnel must be built right beneath a city street. Of course a tunnel of this kind doesn't require what we usually think of as real tunneling, real burrowing through the earth. Its builders can simply remove the street paving for as long as their job lasts, and do their work in the open air.

The First Attempt
to Tunnel Beneath a River

Except for the Euphrates tunnel, no underwater tunnel was ever built, so far as we know, until the nineteenth century. The first one built then, in England, is still used today. It provides passage beneath the River Thames where it flows through London. And it was not done by the cut-and-cover method. It was dug entirely through the earth under the river, and is thus often called the world's first real subaqueous tunnel.

The Thames tunnel wasn't built because people were afraid to cross that river. Thousands were crossing it every day by the early years of the nineteenth century. One especially large group lived in the crowded part of London known as Wapping, along the river's north bank. To reach their jobs at the busy wharves and leather factories of Rotherhithe, on the opposite bank, they had only two possible routes. They could walk or ride about two miles up the river to London Bridge, cross that bridge, and return down along the river to Rotherhithe. Or they could pay whatever fee was demanded by the watermen who rowed people back and forth across the river.

So it is easy to understand why there was a great demand for a faster and easier way to cross the river at Wapping. A bridge there would have to be so high, to allow for ship traffic, that the long slanting roads leading up to it would be extremely costly. A tunnel under the river thus seemed the only solution, and several engineers offered plans for building one.

Among them was Richard Trevithick, a self-educated mining engineer whose steam engine had helped open the way to railroad travel. When a group of businessmen decided that a Thames tunnel would be profitable, they hired him to build it. But Trevithick found that the river bed consisted of nothing but soft earth, clay, loose gravel, silt, and sand. After five years of trying to dig through that kind of material — so different from the rock that tunnelers were familiar with — he gave the job up as hopeless.

The reason for his failure is clear to anyone who has ever tried to dig a tunnel through a little mound of sand. The task seems simple enough at first. You simply scoop out a handful of sand at the base of the mound, and then another and another. You work very carefully, of course. But the stand-up time of sand is so short that your tunnel may collapse, trapping your hand beneath the fallen sand, before you can hole the tunnel through.

After Trevithick's unsuccessful attempt, nobody seemed able to suggest a satisfactory method for doing what he hadn't been able to do. Most people agreed that tunneling through soft material like the Thames riverbed would never be possible.

Marc Brunel and His Shield

One day a man walking across a London shipyard picked up a worm-eaten timber from a ship under repair. And as soon as he looked at it through the magnifying glass he always carried in his pocket, he decided a tunnel under the Thames might be possible after all. His name was Marc Brunel. He and his son, Isambard Brunel, are two of the most famous men in tunneling history.

Born on a prosperous farm in France in 1769, Marc Brunel was always interested in mathematics and mechanical things. He joined the French Royal Navy, to learn such skills as navigation, and spent several years overseas. On his return, in the middle of the French Revolution, he was threatened with death because of his fierce loyalty to the king. He fled from France on a ship bound for the new United States, where he became an American citizen and was soon named New York's chief engineer.

Brunel returned to Europe in 1799, however, to marry an English girl he had fallen in love with years before. And in England, too, his abilities were soon recognized. England's Royal Navy accepted his designs for machines to make the wooden pulleys that hoist and lower ships' sails. He also invented new machines for sawing and bending timber, for knitting stockings, for making sails, and for manufacturing boots for the British army. But he was more interested in inventing machines than in making money from them. In 1821 he was thrown into prison for debt.

By then many of England's leaders believed that their nation's success, in the new world of scientific and industrial progress, depended on men like Brunel. So one of them, the Duke of Wellington, had him released from prison after Brunel promised to remain in England for the rest of his life.

But that takes us ahead of our story. It was in 1815 that Brunel picked up that piece of worm-eaten timber and studied the little worm that had riddled it with holes.

Like almost everyone of that time, Brunel knew that the shipworm, as it is called, destroyed more of England's wooden ships than she lost to her enemies in time of war. But no one had ever learned how a small soft worm could do so much damage. That day Brunel found out.

A shipworm has a hard protective shell on each side of its head. The toothed edges of those shells can cut into wood, producing powder-like tiny shavings. The worm consumes that powder, digests it, and then gives off a substance that forms a hard lining in the tiny tunnel it is digging. A shipworm, in other words, is a remarkably efficient tunnel-digging machine.

Brunel immediately began to design a "machine" that would make use of what he had learned.

The simplest way to think of his invention is to imagine a huge metal can, open at one end. In the closed end of the can — the digging end, which is placed against the tunnel face — there are many small holes, or pockets, each fitted with a tight cover. Inside the can, and protected by it from cave-ins, the tunnel workers stand in front of the holes. Each man uncovers a hole, digs out a small amount of earth, and replaces the cover before more earth can slide through. In this way the first few inches of earth are removed from in front of the can. Jacks then force the can forward those few inches, and the process is repeated over and over.

During each period of digging, workers inside the back end of the can are making a brick — or stone or iron — lining for the tunnel. They put it together directly against the can's inner surface. Thus, when the jacks move the can forward, the newly made lining is left behind. By this method the walls and ceiling of the tunnel are always supported, first by the can, then by the tunnel's own lining.

Brunel called his invention a shield, because it protected both the tunnel builders and the tunnel itself.

His first design for it was a round "can." Later he changed its shape to a rectangle thirty-eight feet wide and twenty-two and a half feet high. It was made of cast iron and weighed eighty tons. Against its closed end, on the inside, were three "shelves" or platforms, each divided into twelve sections. Brunel thus had thirty-six "cells" as he called them, for men to stand in, each facing a covered hole. He believed thirty-six workmen could dig a tunnel at the rate of three feet a day.

The Duke of Wellington and other wealthy men decided that Brunel's shield would make a Thames tunnel possible — and profitable too. They formed a tunnel-building company and hired Brunel as its engineer.

The First Thames Tunnel

By early 1823 Brunel was planning every part of the work ahead. The tunnel was to be wide enough for two brick-lined carriage roads, separated by a row of brick archways. It would be dug from the bottom of a deep shaft he planned to sink close to the Rotherhithe bank of the river. On March 2, 1825, he laid the first brick for the lining of the shaft. The second brick was laid by his nineteen-year-old son, Isambard, who would serve as his assistant on the job.

They laid their bricks on a heavy iron ring enclosing a circle fifty feet in diameter. On that ring workmen then began to build a brick wall three feet thick, braced by iron rods. As this wall grew taller, the earth inside and beneath it was dug out so that the ring

A nine-cell section of Brunel's thirty-six-cell shield used to dig the first tunnel under the Thames River in London. *Drawing courtesy London Transport.*

and its wall sank a few inches each day. By late November of that year the ring was at the bottom of the shaft, fifty feet below the surface, and the shaft was already permanently lined by its three-foot-thick brick wall. Brunel's shield was put together at the bottom of the shaft and the tunneling began. Brunel hoped to complete the tunnel in three years.

Going down the shaft to look at Brunel's tunnel became a popular pastime for Londoners. Visitors to the city often said the tunnel was the first thing they wanted to see. Foreign ambassadors had orders to inspect the tunnel and report on its progress to their own governments. Brunel complained that his numerous guests were a nuisance. They asked a lot of questions, most of which seemed silly to him, but which he had to answer. They got in the way of his workmen and wasted their time. And that time was very valuable. In order to persuade men to work under the river, Brunel had been forced to pay unusually high wages to the three shifts of miners, muckers, and bricklayers he needed to keep the work going on around the clock.

But his employers were collecting a fee from every visitor to the tunnel, and they ignored Brunel's complaints. Every day dozens of sightseers were lowered down the shaft into the tunnel itself.

In spite of everything, however, fourteen feet of tunnel were successfully dug and lined by the end of two months.

Then disaster struck. The river broke through the soft muck of its bottom, pouring thousands of gallons of water through the shield and into the tunnel. Oil lamps and candles were snuffed out. Terrified workmen threshed wildly about in the dark, trying to reach the shaft before they drowned. Somehow every one of them managed to escape to safety. Before the water stopped pouring in it had filled the tunnel and was twelve feet deep in the shaft.

The hole in the river bottom was plugged from above by dropping clay-filled bags into it from barges. The water was pumped out of the tunnel and the shaft. Finally Brunel could get his men back to work.

A month later the river broke through again, and though this time the men didn't panic, the entire time-consuming process of emptying the tunnel had to be repeated.

There were daily problems too. Water always seeped in when a workman uncovered a pocket to dig out a patch of gravel and muck. With the water came the gases and smells of London's sewers, which emptied into the Thames. Men took sick and some were temporarily blinded. Eventually Marc Brunel himself became so ill that he never fully recovered. His son had to take his place as chief engineer.

From then on young Isambard Brunel was at the tunnel day and night, sometimes snatching only a few hours of sleep a week.

One day, when the tunneling had been going on for about a year and a half, the river poured into the tunnel once more. Again everyone escaped to safety, and again bags of clay were dropped into the hole from above. But this time young Brunel was worried about the construction of the shield. So he lowered a small boat into the shaft and waited until the water level had dropped a few feet beneath the tunnel's ceiling. Then he got into the boat and, pushing on the ceiling with his hands, set off on a tour of inspection. He finally reached the shield and found it undamaged. The tedious job of pumping went on, and after several months the crews were again back at work.

Then, only a few months later, the tunnel was once more flooded. That time six men drowned in the stinking water, and young Brunel was badly injured. Again the dreary task of pumping began. But by the time it was finished, the last of the company's funds had been spent. To the Brunels' shock and utter dismay, they were ordered to wall off the partly finished tunnel and abandon it.

It remained sealed for seven years — years during which young Brunel became a leader in England's rush to build railroads and steamships. In 1834, when the tunnel company received a loan from the government, and the tunnel could be opened up again, other engineers carried forward the elder Brunel's project.

The work on it went on for seven more years, interrupted by five serious breaks. More workers were blinded. More became sick or were injured. But despite its hazards the tunnel continued to attract some nine hundred visitors every week.

Finally the great day arrived. On March 25, 1842, the Thames Tunnel was officially opened. Young Brunel was there, of course, and so was his ailing father, recently knighted by Queen Victoria. It was a splendid occasion. And before another day had passed, fifty thousand people had walked through Brunel's famous tunnel.

Those walkers could reach the tunnel by descending the original shaft on the Rotherhithe side of the river, or the one built afterward at Wapping on the opposite side. But there were no road connections to the tunnel, to permit carriages and carts to use it. The tunnel company couldn't afford to build them. And the shillings collected from those who walked through the vast two-road tunnel, in the following years, were not enough to keep it in repair.

Some said the only person who ever profited from the tunnel was the man who sold souvenir handkerchiefs at one entrance. On the day Queen Victoria arrived for a visit, he spread his whole stock on the floor for her party to walk on. Then he charged six times his usual price for handkerchiefs he said had been touched by the royal feet.

Eventually the tunnel was being used chiefly by homeless men, who took shelter in it on rainy nights. But in 1865 it was bought by the East London Railway Company and soon it took on a new life. It became one of the many underwater tunnels now used by trains.

Trainloads of job-seekers and sightseers were by then pouring into most big cities every day. By the 1860s city streets were clogged with horse-drawn traffic. A man could arrive in London's Padding-

Pedestrians using Brunel's tunnel to walk under the Thames River. *Drawing courtesy London Transport.*

ton Station, for example, from his village some fifty miles away, in about two hours. But he might have to spend several additional hours traveling the three miles to Charing Cross, in the heart of the city.

Therefore there had been great rejoicing in 1863, when a short tunnel was built in London to extend the railway line from Paddington Station to the city's center. The twenty-minute ride through that tunnel, behind a smoke-belching steam locomotive, was not very pleasant. But it proved that traveling through a city could be as swift as traveling to it. People began to dream of what we call subways — what Londoners call undergrounds — beneath all the big cities of the world.

Engineers realized from the start that — since rivers flow through so many large cities — almost every big-city subway would have to cross over water or go beneath it. And since it was clear

A crowded London Street in the 1870s, as seen by the famous French artist Gustave Doré.

that an underwater tunnel would be the best solution in many cases, more attention began to be paid to such tunnels.

Peter Barlow
and James Henry Greathead

Two Londoners developed a really practical method for building those underwater subway tunnels. One was the English-born engineer Peter W. Barlow. The other, James Henry Greathead, had come to London to serve as Barlow's apprentice. Greathead had been born in Britain's Cape Colony, now South Africa.

Barlow wanted to attempt another tunnel under the Thames. It would be far smaller than the Brunels', but he hoped it would serve as a pattern for tunnels big enough to carry trains. He planned to use Brunel's idea of a shield, but he thought his would be easier to push forward because it would be round — the shape Brunel had first thought of. And Barlow planned to line his tunnel with cast iron — and that too was an idea Brunel had once considered.

Barlow's lining would be brought into the tunnel in the form of cast iron rings cut into segments. The segments of each ring were to be put together inside the tunnel. Then, by bolting each new ring to the one before it, a solid cast-iron tube would be formed. The small space left between the iron tunnel lining and the surrounding earth would be filled by a special liquid squirted through small holes in the lining. The holes could be quickly plugged up after enough liquid had been forced through them. That liquid would harden to form a kind of cement coating around the outside of the iron tube.

Barlow raised the money for his experimental tunnel and then could find no one to build it. Every building contractor he talked to refused to risk the kind of disasters the Brunels had encountered. So when his twenty-five-year-old apprentice offered to tackle the job, Barlow was delighted.

Young Greathead started work on the tunnel in 1869. He finished it within a single year. Its little twelve-passenger car, pulled back and forth by cables, was soon given up. But the tunnel did serve as a pattern for the future, as Barlow had hoped. One reason for that was the new tunneling techniques Greathead developed. He devised machinery, for example, to lift and fasten together the heavy cast-iron ring segments. Most important of all, he used compressed air in the working space behind the shield. If the pressure of the air there was made equal to the pressure of the material outside the shield, silt and water would not pour through the shield's pockets when they were opened.

To keep the air pressure in Greathead's tunnel from leaking away, workers had to enter it through an airtight room called an air lock. Once they were inside the air lock, the outer door was closed behind them, and air was pumped into the lock. After the pressure in the lock was raised to equal the pressure of the air in

Putting together the cast-iron rings that lined Barlow's small 1869 tunnel under the Thames. *Drawing courtesy London Transport.*

the workspace beyond, the inner door was opened to admit them to the tunnel itself.

Greathead used his new method to build the world's first real subway of any length. Its double line of cast-iron "tubes," ten and a half feet in diameter, ran for three and a half miles beneath London's streets and under the Thames. And its trains ran on the newly developed power of electricity. Those who made the first trip through it, in March 1890, praised the smoke-free journey for its "perfect comfort and atmosphere." Greathead himself was especially proud that no accidents of any kind had occurred during the tunnel construction.

Deeper Underwater Tunnels and Their Dangers

Greathead's method was soon being successfully used for the building of other underwater tunnels. Like the London subway, they were all built so close to the surface that only low air pressures were needed. But when deeper underwater tunnels were attempted, greater air pressures had to be used to equal the greater pressure from the material outside. Many workers then developed sudden and severe pains. Some died in agony; others were crippled for life.

For some time no one understood what caused that illness, which came to be known as the bends, and which also endangers deep-sea divers. It occurs because the amount of nitrogen in the blood increases when the body is under pressure. The higher the pressure, the greater the increase. Then, if heavy pressure is suddenly reduced — if a diver is raised up quickly from deep water, for example — bubbles of nitrogen explode in the blood vessels and damage the body's tissues.

Once the cause of the bends was known, laws were passed to protect tunnelers from the dread disease. Those laws limit the time a man is allowed to work under heavy pressure. They also provide him with enough time to safely "decompress" in the air lock, where pressure can gradually be reduced to normal. Workers in some deep tunnels are now allowed to remain on the job for only an hour a day, and must spend six hours in decompression. This is one reason for the high cost of modern deep underwater tunnel building.

In 1874, before those laws were passed, work started on twin train tunnels under the Hudson River, where that river runs between New York City and New Jersey. The engineer who contracted to do the job, DeWitt Clinton Haskins, was a successful railway builder from California. The method he planned to use was one he said he had invented. It did not use an "expensive" shield, as he put it. Instead it used air pressure alone "to resist the caving in of the wall or the infiltrations of water, until the masonry wall is completed."

Haskins started by digging a shaft on the New Jersey shore, from which the first of the two tunnels would be built. Legal problems halted the project even before the shaft was finished. Five years later Haskins returned to the job, and managed to dig through almost half a mile of silt without using a shield. But every month the bends claimed the life of at least one "sandhog," as an American underwater tunneler had come to be called. And Haskins's progress was also seriously slowed by "blowouts."

A blowout occurs when compressed air seeps out through a tunnel wall. If the hole through which it escapes is noticed in time, it can sometimes be plugged up before serious damage is done. When the air seepage can't be stopped, however, the results are often fatal to anyone in the tunnel at the time. The seeping air forms a bubble, which bursts with the force of an explosion. And as that explosion draws more compressed air out of the tunnel in a great rush, water and silt pour in. Twenty men were drowned in just one of the floods caused by blowouts in the Hudson River tunnel.

Haskins's money ran out not long after that tragedy, and the two Hudson River tunnels he had started were abandoned. Several years later an English company agreed to finish them, and by using Greathead's shield it made great progress. But it, too, ran out of money, and had to give up the job, even though one of the tunnels was almost finished. Ten years later the work was resumed, this time by a new American company with sound financial backing.

Again shields were used, and almost immediately the forward movement of one of them was halted by an unexpected obstacle: it had come up against a reef of rock. The only method anyone could think of for getting past that barrier was to blast it out of the way. Rock blasting had never before been attempted in an underwater tunnel, and would clearly be dangerous there. But unless it was attempted, the Hudson tunnels would remain incomplete and useless.

So small holes were drilled in the rock, by men working through the pockets in the shield, and small amounts of blasting powder were exploded inside them. The feeble blasts that resulted did no harm to the workers or the tunnel itself. They also shattered very little rock. But no one dared risk larger blasts, and the same procedure was therefore repeated hour after hour, day after day. Four-

This drawing, which appeared in the *Scientific American* of November 1890, shows men at work on the first tunnel dug under the Hudson River. Through the openings in the shield, the sandhogs dug out the muck and silt, which was carried away in mule-drawn carts. The man on the platform operates the "erector" arm, which lifts iron segments of the tunnel lining in place so that they can be bolted together to form a ring. *Drawing courtesy Port Authority of New York and New Jersey.*

teen months passed before the rock reef was finally broken through.

Not long afterward, in 1904, and thirty years after Haskins had started the project, the first tunnel under the Hudson was completed. Its twin was finished four years later. Once, the Hudson could be crossed only by a slow ferry ride. Now that trip could be made in only a few minutes on the tunnel-traveling trains of the Hudson and Manhattan Railroad. Operated today by the joint New York–New Jersey Port Authority, the tunnels now form part of the transport organization called PATH, from the initials of the Port Authority Trans-Hudson System.

One of the several tunnels later built under the Hudson is the famous two-tube mile-and-a-half Holland Tunnel. When it was finished in 1927 it was the world's longest underwater tunnel, and the first one ever built for the use of cars, trucks, and buses. Its engineer, brilliant young Clifford M. Holland, had realized that it would have to have a special ventilation system to remove the dangerous exhaust fumes from automobile engines. The one he planned was designed only after elaborate tests had been made. It still works well today and has been a model for other such systems. Its eighty-four immense fans are housed in four huge buildings, two on each side of the river. They can change the air throughout the entire tunnel every ninety seconds.

The tunnel's name honors its engineer. Holland had died, exhausted by overwork, just two days before the first of his tunnels was holed through. He was forty-one years old.

Hudson River sandhogs, tunneling through silt, made two useful discoveries. One group found that it was sometimes possible to open a few pockets in a shield and — instead of scooping out the silt — simply let it ooze through the openings like toothpaste oozing out of a tube. Another group learned that in some places silt offered so little resistance that a shield could be jacked forward through it without either digging it out or letting it ooze through the pockets. Both methods have since saved a good deal of time and money.

The heavy traffic in and around New York City has required tunnels under other bodies of water, too. They were built to connect the island of Manhattan, one of the city's five boroughs, with three of its other boroughs — Brooklyn, Queens, and the Bronx. And during the construction of a subway tunnel under the East River, between Manhattan and Brooklyn, a strange story was added to tunneling history.

One day, when eight men were at work in the tunnel's shield, a leak occurred. A sandhog named Richard Creegan tried to plug it up with a bale of the hay kept on hand for just such emergencies. But suddenly the force of the compressed air blew Creegan himself up into the hole. For a moment he was caught, his legs still dangling

A policeman at his post in the Holland Tunnel under the Hudson River. Eighty-four immense fans keep the air safe to breathe despite the endless flow of traffic. *Photograph courtesy Port Authority of New York and New Jersey.*

inside the tunnel, his head in the silt above it. Then, before other sandhogs had time to reach him, the air pressure shot him upward out of sight. And on up he went, through the silt and through fifteen feet of water, to pop up above the surface of the river. Two men in a boat nearby, astounded by his sudden appearance, managed to haul him to safety. And Creegan lived to tell the tale that sandhogs still repeat today.

Japan's Seikan Tunnel

During the first sixty years of the twentieth century, underwater tunnels of considerable length were built in almost every part of the world. Then, in 1963, Japan announced plans for her Seikan Tunnel, which would be the longest tunnel of any kind ever built. It would stretch for thirty-three and a half miles end to end, linking together the two largest of Japan's major islands, Honshu and Hokkaido. Its fourteen-and-a-half-mile central section, to be dug beneath Tsugaru Strait, would be by far the longest underwater tunnel in the world.

The cost of the Seikan Tunnel would obviously be enormous, but there were good reasons for building it. Honshu, Japan's chief island, is crowded with industries and big cities, including the nation's capital, Tokyo. Its huge population needs more living space, and it must import most of the raw materials its industries use. Hokkaido, on the other hand, has empty space where new settlers

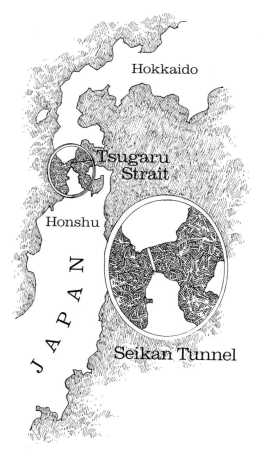

The Tsugaru Strait runs between the Japanese islands of Hokkaido and Honshu.

would be welcome, and much of the coal, lumber, fish, and other natural resources Honshu needs. But transferring people and goods from one island to the other has never been easy.

Transportation by air for such heavy loads as coal is too expensive to be practical. Transportation by sea is both slow and dangerous. Tsugaru Strait is one of the most treacherous bodies of water in the northern Pacific. Severe storms there halt the regular ferry service as often as eighty times a year. One vessel, struck by a typhoon, went down with a loss of 1,172 lives. So a swift, safe, and dependable passage between the two islands would solve one of Japan's most serious problems.

Seikan Tunnel — a railroad tunnel — was to be built by Japan's nationally owned railway system, whose engineers had long experience with rock tunneling. But no one could foresee what the tunnelers would have to dig through under the seabed of Tsugaru Strait. A careful survey of the territory was the first step. That survey went on for twenty-five years. The engineers used submarines to inspect the seabed. They used dredges to bring up samples of the bed for scientific testing. They used sound waves to determine what lay deep beneath the seabed. The plans that were finally completed called for one large tunnel and two smaller ones to be dug about three hundred feet below the bottom of the Strait.

The large tunnel would be for the trains. Parallel to it, and about a hundred feet away, there would be a smaller service tunnel. The third, a pilot tunnel the same size as the service tunnel, was to be constructed between the first two, but below them. Work on all three would go on at the same time, but the pilot tunnel was to advance faster than the other two. It would thus allow the engineers to determine what problems they would encounter. And cross tunnels would be built, connecting the main tunnel with the service tunnel, so that the smaller one could be used for ventilation, for bringing in supplies, and for hauling out muck.

By the time the actual digging started in 1971, the engineers knew what a difficult job they faced. For one thing, the workers would be under such pressure, at three hundred feet below the sea floor, that they could work only one hour out of each eight-hour day. For another thing, the area of the Strait is volcanic and a likely site of earthquakes, because nine fault zones run through it. In a fault zone the plates that form the earth's crust are shifting and moving against one another. Cracks and openings in the rock let water seep through. So blowouts and floods were expected, and did prove a constant hindrance to the work. During one blowout, water poured into the tunnel at a rate of forty tons a minute. At one place the work proceeded so slowly that it took four months to advance the tunnel forty feet.

Under the middle of the Strait the tunnelers ran into an area of soft, sandy muck. The engineers had to find a way of hardening that muck so that it wouldn't cave in as the tunnelers dug through it. They solved that problem by using high-pressure pumps to inject a liquid mixture of cement and chemicals into the muck, for a distance of two hundred feet ahead of the shield. When that mixture hardened, it turned the soft muck into a concrete-like mass which the miners could safely drill through.

Slowly the work progressed. On January 27, 1983, Japan's prime minister pressed the button in his Tokyo office that set off the final blast to hole through the pilot tunnel. After another two years, with the service tunnel by then completed, the thirty-five-foot-wide main tunnel was finally holed through. That dramatic event occurred on March 16, 1985, to the wild cheers of the triumphant tunnelers.

The toughest and most dangerous part of building the world's longest tunnel had been finished. The job had lasted over fifteen years and cost the lives of thirty-four men.

Installing the tracks, the electrical systems, and the other equipment the railroad would need was expected to take at least another two or three years. But before the 1990s arrived, the Japanese engineers believed, Japan's two main islands would be safely connected by an undersea rail line.

The English Channel Tunnel

While the record-breaking Seikan Tunnel was being built, people were talking — as people had talked off and on for at least one hundred and eighty years — about building a tunnel under the English Channel. This often choppy body of water between England and France is twenty-two and a quarter miles wide at its narrowest point — even wider than the Tsugaru Strait.

A French engineer first suggested the idea of a cross-channel tunnel to his emperor in 1802, but Napoleon wasn't interested. Thirty years later another French engineer weighted himself with rocks and twice dove a hundred feet into the Channel to study its bottom. Satisfied with what he found there, he spent his large fortune and most of the rest of his life devising Channel-tunnel schemes. None of them was ever attempted.

Other engineers, some French, some English, brought forth their own schemes as time went by. Isambard Brunel was one of the notable Englishmen who encouraged them. Twice during the late nineteenth century a tunnel was actually begun. Shafts were dug on both shores. Pilot tunnels were started. But both projects were abandoned, the second one at the demand of British military officers. They insisted that a tunnel would provide too easy a route for any future enemy intent on invading England.

When work on one more tunnel attempt was stopped in 1975 because of lack of funds, a short stretch of tunnel had already been dug near the Channel port city of Dover. Its entrance was closed, and wild blackberry vines grew over the supply tracks leading up to it. But it is inspected regularly and kept in good condition in case money for restarting this particular project is ever found. And plans are still made, and remade, for other versions of a Channel tunnel, or Chunnel, as it has been nicknamed.

Most of those plans call for a bored tunnel carrying one or two railroad tracks. An especially ambitious design is for a tunnel large enough for two railroad tracks and two automobile lanes as well. But one of the newer plans would give up the idea of boring in favor of the trench, or "build-and-sink" method, which has a good deal in common with the long-used cut-and-cover method.

The build-and-sink method requires, first, digging a trench in the seabed to hold the tunnel structure. That structure is built on land, in sections. Each section is sealed at both ends, towed out to sea, flooded, and allowed to sink into the trench. When divers have fastened the sections together, the whole tunnel structure is covered with a heavy layer of rocks and gravel, and then pumped dry.

This method has already been used for several fairly long underwater tunnels. One of them, under Chesapeake Bay between Maryland and Virginia, forms part of a major American coastal highway. During a severe storm, while that tunnel was being built, one section of the tube was shifted out of the trench. Getting it back into place was a costly and dangerous task.

One of the thirty-two steel and concrete sections used in the construction of the Fort McHenry Tunnel in Baltimore, Maryland. The sections were floated out into Baltimore Harbor, sunk into a prepared trench in the harbor bottom, and welded together under water to complete the 7,200-foot-long vehicular tunnel. *Photograph courtesy Bethlehem Steel Corporation.*

The build-and-sink method, as that accident and others have proved, is not foolproof. But no foolproof method has yet been developed — and perhaps none ever will be — for building a safe passage under water from one place to another.

5.
Tunnels beneath Cities:
Subways

James Henry Greathead began talking about the future of underground travel as soon as he finished that second little tunnel under the Thames. He said London should have a whole system of subways, and that if it was built fifty feet or more below the surface, it wouldn't disturb buildings or the city's water and sewer lines.

London Leads the Way

Government officials agreed that Greathead's plan would solve the problem of London's increasingly traffic-jammed streets. City property owners were delighted with the plan, too. As owners of the soil beneath the surface of their land — they said they owned it all the way down to the center of the earth — they expected to be well paid for the right to tunnel through it. At first their demand seemed reasonable enough. But they asked such huge prices for tunneling rights that the plan had to be abandoned as too costly.

Greathead then made a new suggestion. What about tunneling only beneath public streets? he said.

This brought up new questions: Who owned the earth under

London's streets? Did it belong to the city? And if so, could the city demand payment for any tunneling done through it?

In 1884 the British Parliament provided the answers. Its Subway Act ruled that the city did own the earth under its streets, and that subways could be built there without payment of fees because subways would be for the public's good.

Greathead was finally free to start work on London's first real subway. It was that three-and-a-half-mile double tube already described, which opened in March of 1890. Much of it was built by the cut-and-cover method, with little difficulty, and its new electrically powered trains increased enthusiasm for swift underground travel. From then on more subways were built, stretching out toward one corner of London after another.

Subways were being talked about in other European capitals too.

Paris was one of them. Her population had recently tripled and her streets, on both sides of the River Seine, were as crowded as London's. But some Parisians objected to the very idea of subways.

The cut-and-cover method was used to build many of the early subways. Workmen here are building a part of London's underground. *Photograph courtesy London Transport.*

They might do for the British, one man said, because those people were "used to the fogs of London." But, he added, Parisians were "people of the sun" and preferred to travel in its light. He was one of the many who declared that Paris should have elevated railways running on tracks lifted high into the air.

Even those Parisians who did want subways disagreed over whether they should be controlled by the government of Paris or the government of France. For years the arguments went on. No elevated tracks were built, and no subways either.

In the meantime French business and industrial leaders were planning a great International Exposition to be held in Paris in 1900. They remembered that foreigners visiting a similar exposition, in 1867, had complained loudly about the city's miserably crowded streets. They expected even louder complaints in 1900, if no improvements had been made by then. One reason for this was that three other European cities already had, or were about to have, some form of rapid transit, as the new methods of traveling were called.

Glasgow, in Scotland, a much smaller city than Paris, had had a little cable-car subway since 1886. Budapest, Hungary's capital, would soon open her trolley tunnel. And the subway network of London, long the rival of Paris, was now growing steadily.

Paris Takes
the Underground Route

The disagreements over any kind of rapid transit for Paris finally came to an end in 1895, largely to please the Exposition planners. Underground routes won out over elevated railroads. The French government agreed to let Paris control them. A subway system was soon devised that would serve the entire city. Parisians believed it would be far better than the London network, which had been started with no overall plan. And the Paris subway entrances were to be designed in the newest artistic style, to remind visitors that they were in the recognized capital of the world of art.

In 1898 work started on what Parisians have always called their Métro. The name is an abbreviation of Chemin de Fer Métropolitain, or Metropolitan Railway of Paris.

Its engineer made great use of the cut-and-cover method, which usually presents fewer problems than deep tunneling. But he still faced difficulties. In one patch of quicksand, huge masonry columns had to be built deep underground, to support the subway. Marshy ground along the River Seine had to be frozen hard before it could be dug without disastrous cave-ins. Costly refrigerating plants had to be built to make that possible. And some of the famous sewers of Paris had to be shifted to make room for these new tunnels.

French archaeologists, like those in England, watched the digging with great interest. In each city important finds were made underground. Among them were coins and mosaic pavements that dated back two thousand years, to the time when both London and Paris were Roman settlements.

But when the first line of the Paris Métro opened, in July 1900, local newspapers scarcely mentioned it. Perhaps that was because the Exposition of 1900, already underway, claimed everyone's attention. Or perhaps, as a writer later suggested, it was because Parisians had waited so long for a subway that they couldn't believe it did finally exist.

New York
Considers Underground Travel

In the meantime, in New York City, a different story had been unfolding. There, more than half a century earlier, a slight, frail, intense young man had suggested a plan for an underground route beneath Broadway, the most crowded of all the city's crowded streets. He was twenty-three-year-old Alfred Ely Beach, owner and publisher of a new magazine, the *Scientific American.*

Beach used his magazine as if he were a teacher with half the world as his classroom. (He brought out a Spanish edition too, so that it could be read in Central and South America.) He wanted to tell everyone about the scientific and industrial worlds that were then exploding with new developments. He described each important new invention — he was an inventor himself, of a typewriter among other things. And he encouraged his readers to explore, in his pages, such rapidly growing fields as engineering, chemistry, and electricity.

To Beach, the overcrowded streets of New York were a problem that could be solved by using the latest scientific and engineering knowledge. He knew Brunel had made use of such knowledge to tunnel under the Thames. The plan he proposed in 1849 was to "tunnel Broadway through the whole length, with openings and stairways at every corner. This subterranean passage is to be laid down with double track, with a road for foot passengers on either side — the whole to be brilliantly lit with gas." His horse-drawn cars, he said, would "stop ten seconds at every corner — thus performing the trip up and down, including stops, in about an hour."

Beach's plan was applauded by people who daily rode the city's horse-drawn omnibuses and street railway cars. They had long complained of being packed into those vehicles "like sardines." More and faster public transportation was needed, they said, especially on busy Broadway. And if it was underground, they pointed out, so much the better, since crossing Broadway already was "as much as your life is worth."

But sober businessmen feared that a tunnel beneath a traffic-laden street would cause the street to collapse, along with all the buildings on either side of it. Owners of buildings along Broadway were among those who spoke out most strongly about that danger.

One other man, William Marcy Tweed, also opposed Beach's plan, and his opposition alone was enough to destroy its chances. Tweed's official title was that of city commissioner of public works. But "Boss" Tweed, as he was known, actually controlled almost everything that went on in the city and in the state legislature, too. In return for enormous bribes, for example, he had given certain companies the exclusive right to operate New York's horse-drawn omnibuses and railway cars. No other form of transportation, and no other transport companies, would be allowed to exist in the city as long as "Boss" Tweed remained in power.

Mr. Beach
Outwits "Boss" Tweed

Beach refused to be discouraged. He became even more enthusiastic about the possibilities of underground travel when he learned about European experiments with a "pneumatic" tube. Inside such a tube, he had read, people could travel by air pressure — swiftly, silently, and without smoke.

Beach promptly built his own model of such a tube. It was about one hundred feet long, and the little ten-passenger car inside it was blown from one end of the tube to the other by a powerful fan. He exhibited his tube to New Yorkers at an industrial fair in 1867, and a hundred thousand people were delighted with their ride in it.

Then Beach, setting himself up as the Beach Pneumatic Transport Company, sought a charter for building a pair of underground pneumatic tubes. They would deliver letters and packages to the city's main post office, he explained, with "almost the speed of the telegraph." Each tube would be four and a half feet in diameter.

Tweed could see no threat in a pair of mail tubes. He permitted Beach to receive his charter. Tweed didn't even object to Beach's last-minute request: that he be allowed to build one larger tube, inside of which the two small ones could be installed. Such a plan, Beach had claimed, would save money.

Some twenty years had gone by since Beach first suggested a subway for New York. Now he wasted no time in seizing the opportunity he had contrived to build one without "Boss" Tweed's knowledge. He also kept his project just as secret from the businessmen and property owners who had always expressed worry about the danger of underground tunneling.

From a merchant friend, the owner of a large clothing store at the corner of Broadway and Warren Street, Beach obtained his starting point. In the basement of that handsome marble building, at a level more than twenty feet below the street, Beach set a small crew to work. Like Brunel, he had put his son in charge of what he hoped would be another history-making tunnel. And the digging was to be done by means of a shield Beach had built, copied largely after Brunel's model.

The crew worked only at night. The wheels of its carts, in which the dug-out soil was carried away, were muffled in cloth so that they made no noise over the cobblestoned streets. The shield proved efficient. It ate steadily away at the earth ahead of it, as it was jacked forward on a curve to a spot under the center of Broadway, and then turned to continue along beneath that wide thoroughfare.

The work went quickly — until the night young Fred Beach found a wall of stone blocking the way of the shield. He knew it could not be the foundation of an existing building, because there was nothing above it except the Broadway pavement. But it might now be an important support of the street above. To destroy it could bring about the collapse that had so often been predicted as the result of under-street tunneling. To leave it standing would mean bringing the tunnel to a halt.

Fred Beach could not take such a heavy responsibility on his own shoulders. He drove to his father's home, some blocks away, and wakened him. Beach dressed hastily, drove to the store, descended to its basement, and hurried along the tunnel until he reached the shield.

Carefully he studied the well-fitted stones just beyond it. He tapped them, one after the other.

"Remove them," he said finally.

And so, with great caution, the stones were loosened and pulled out of their place to be carted away.

The wall of earth beyond them was solid. The pavement did not sag or crack above it. The work went on.

At the end of fifty-eight nights the crew had dug a tunnel 312 feet long. Part of it was lined with white-painted brick, part with iron rings bolted together. Beach installed gaslights along its walls. He had a huge fan, turned by a hundred-horsepower steam engine, set up at one end of the tunnel. He had tracks laid down for the handsomely upholstered twenty-two-passenger car he had ordered.

Then Beach furnished a large space directly under the sidewalk, at the Warren Street end of the tunnel, with chairs and couches. He hung chandeliers from the ceiling and put mirrors and paintings on the walls. he brought in a grandfather clock and a grand piano. He had a fountain installed, and a goldfish pond. It was to be his subway waiting room, and he wanted it to be "cozy," he said, for his women passengers.

On February 20, 1870, Beach invited guests to inspect what he had built. They were dazzled by the splendor of the waiting room. They were enchanted by their ride in the elegant car, which was blown gently along its tracks by the huge fan. When the car reached the far end of the tunnel, the fan was reversed and gently sucked the car back to its starting point.

Newspapers described the event with astonishment.

"A FASHIONABLE RECEPTION HELD IN THE BOWELS OF THE EARTH!" read one headline. The waiting room was described in detail. The car, one story said, was sent "skimming along the tracks like a sail before the wind."

One of the most popular magazines of the day, *Leslie's Illustrated Weekly,* sent artists into the tunnel to make the drawings which were used as illustrations in its article called "The Broadway Pneumatic Tunnel." According to the article, the tunnel was part of the "shell" or outer tunnel, which had been built to enclose two mail-carrying tubes. But, the article went on, since the tunnel "proves to be strong enough and large enough for the transit of passengers, it is to be hoped that the company will be compelled by law to . . . open their tunnel for passenger traffic."

Many people enthusiastically agreed with the magazine. And what it was advising, of course, was exactly what Beach himself had had in mind from the start. His trick had worked.

He had proved that it was possible to tunnel under a street without harming the street above or the buildings beside it.

And he had built a subway — in spite of "Boss" Tweed. Every day people were hurrying down into the clothing store basement to pay twenty-five cents to ride in the little car that traveled underground. (The money went to charity, since Beach had no charter to collect passenger fares — and hadn't in any case built his subway to make a fortune.) Every day more people were talking, as Beach himself had talked for years, about the time when underground

There were soft seats and table lamps in Beach's air-driven car in New York's first subway. *Drawing from* Frank Leslie's Illustrated Weekly.

tracks would run all the way from one end of Broadway to the other.

"Boss" Tweed, of course, was furious. He immediately filed a suit against Beach. But Tweed's grip on the city and the state of New York was finally being loosened by determined government reformers. Tweed lost his suit. Soon he was facing the charges that would bring about his downfall. Convicted of perjury and of theft, the once powerful Tweed ended his career in prison.

Then, for a brief period, many important New Yorkers seemed eager to invest in Beach's plan for a citywide pneumatic subway. But before they could raise sufficient funds, a severe financial depression struck the entire country. Banks, factories, and railroads went bankrupt. No money was available for any new venture. Beach sadly gave the order to seal up the brightly lit little tunnel that had given him so much satisfaction, and that had seemed for a while the beginning of a solution to New York's traffic problem.

When that panic of the 1870s had passed, and New York did finally acquire a new means of transportation, it took the form of elevated trains. By 1878 elevated tracks above four of the city's major avenues were darkening the pavements below. "They turn our streets into tunnels," some people complained.

But those elevated trains soon became as crowded as the old horse cars had been, and once again subways were proposed. In 1891 a Rapid Transit Commission was appointed to see that they were built. Their chief engineer, the young but experienced William Parsons, set off to examine Europe's subways before drawing up his own plans.

First Subways in the United States

Parsons's plans for New York were still not complete when, in 1897, Boston opened North America's first subway.

That electrically powered line had been built by the cut-and-cover method but, like every subway in the world, it had had its problems. One arose because part of the line ran beneath Boston's famous old colonial burying ground, and 910 bodies had to be moved to make room for it.

New Yorkers had lost their chance to have America's first subway, but they made a great fuss over the ground-breaking ceremony for their own, on March 24, 1900. The silver spade that was used had been made by Tiffany, the world-famous jeweler. Whistles blew from factories and harbor vessels. That night twenty-five thousand people watched a glorious fireworks display.

The work that began that day continued steadily for over four years. Tunnels had to be dug under the Harlem River and through the rocky cliffs at the northern end of Manhattan. But most of the subway was built by cut-and-cover. Underground springs and streams did cause problems. So did shoppers and shopkeepers, angry over the torn-up streets. But everyone was interested when the tunnelers uncovered *The Tiger,* a Dutch ship that had burned and sank in 1613, and when several huge mastodon bones were found.

A few years later New York subway builders made another discovery. One day in 1912 workers on a new Broadway subway line suddenly broke into an old tunnel, and realized they had "discovered" the experimental subway Beach had built some forty years earlier. By then engineers were in agreement that Beach's plan — to drive subway cars by powerful fans — would never have been practical. But they also agreed that Beach had played an important part in subway history. So a section of his tunnel was made part of the City Hall Station on the new subway. And on that station's wall, today, a plaque names Alfred Ely Beach as the father of the city's subway system.

Subways for the World

The subways of New York, Paris, and London continued to grow, interrupted only by World War I. After that war subways were started in many other cities too. Some were built deep in the earth, with one track underneath another, and this required new methods for supporting the upper tracks and the buildings towering over them. Some had lengthy underwater sections. San Francisco's transport system — called BART from the initials of the Bay Area Rapid Transit — became immediately famous because of its 3.6-mile tube beneath San Francisco Bay. That tube was the world's longest and deepest underwater tunnel until Japan built her Seikan Tunnel under the Tsugaru Strait.

Cities tried to outdo each other in efficient and comfortable

Subway stations in some cities are decorated with great care. This one, at Paris's Louvre Museum, displays works of art for which the museum is famous. *Photograph by Sam Epstein.*

subway service. In Paris and Montreal, for example, riders on rubber-tired trains were spared the ear-splitting noise New Yorkers complained of. In the completely computerized system in Washington, D.C., closed-circuit TV cameras guard against crime.

Cities have also competed in the size and splendor of their underground stations. Tokyo's are very elaborately decorated. So are those of Moscow, where each one honors a Russian hero or a famous event in Russian history. Mexico City's brightly colored stations also mark historic events.

Today, in many cities, at least one subway station has been expanded into a huge shopping and entertainment center. One of the several such centers in Paris has seven levels, or floors, served by seventy-three escalators. In Montreal, people can stroll through the nearly five miles of corridors and plazas of a "subterranean metropolis." There, a reporter wrote, they can shop, dine, or be entertained "for a week or month without visiting the same place twice. Or setting foot outside."

A Plan for a Future Subway?

Subways have clearly changed in many ways since the day in 1843 when Queen Victoria inspected the four-hundred-yard-long tunnel the Brunels had built under the Thames. Some scientists say, however, that the development of subways has just begun.

In 1978 one of them, Dr. Robert Salter, suggested that future subway tracks may lie deep beneath the earth, perhaps as much as a mile below the surface. Their trains, Dr. Salter said, running in a tube almost free of air, and supported and driven by electromagnetic waves, could reach speeds of thousands of miles an hour. They could, for example, travel from one coast of the United States to the other — from San Francisco, say, to New York — in about twenty minutes.

He adds that this high-speed system, which he calls Planetran, may not be built for a hundred years, and may never be built at all. But Dr. Salter also insists that it could be built by techniques already in use, or already being developed. And it does seem likely that if Alfred Ely Beach were alive today, he would be writing an article about Planetran for the *Scientific American*.

6.
Pathways to Freedom:
Escape Tunnels

Tunnels have been used to escape from places as long as there have been places to escape from. Tunnels have also been used to get into protected places as long as there have been such places that people wanted to get into.

The Bible tells the story of how the walls of Jericho fell down at the blast of trumpets, allowing Joshua to capture the city. Some modern engineers believe that underground digging was the real reason for the collapse of those walls. They know that in the days before armies had cannons or bombs, one of the easiest ways to destroy a city's walls was to tunnel under them.

An attacking army usually began its tunnel some distance outside the walls, beyond sight of the city's defenders. The tunnel began as a narrow passage, which continued until it was almost under a section of the wall. There, supported by timbers to prevent its immediate collapse under the wall's weight, the tunnel was widened and spread out to left and right. As soon as it had been extended beneath a considerable portion of the wall, the tunnelers set the supporting timbers afire and hastily retreated.

When the timbers burned and collapsed, the wall above them collapsed too. The attacking army could then rush over the crumbled remains of the wall into the city itself.

Digging a tunnel of that kind had its difficulties and dangers.

But they were probably less than those faced by captured soldiers attempting to tunnel out of their wartime prison. Stories about those desperate and often despairing tunnelers have been told and retold. One of them is about Union officers captured by the Confederates, during the bloody Civil War that almost destroyed the United States in the 1860s. Those officers dug a tunnel in the hope of escaping from Libby Prison in Richmond, Virginia.

The Libby Prison Escape Tunnel

Living conditions for the twelve hundred men confined in Libby Prison early in 1864 were no worse than those in many other Civil War prisons. Their rations were scanty and sometimes unfit to eat. There was no glass in their barred windows to keep out the winter chill. They slept on the floor, on straw, in whatever clothes they possessed.

Their three-storied brick prison had been a warehouse before the war. Their quarters were its two upper floors and a kitchen on the floor below, where they did their own cooking. They were never allowed to enter any other part of the building, or to leave the building itself, except under guard. The yard around the prison was not walled, but it was brightly gas-lit after dark, and any unguarded prisoner who appeared in it could expect to be shot on sight.

The two men who first decided to attempt escape from Libby Prison were Colonel Thomas E. Rose of Pennsylvania and Major A. G. Hamilton, a Kentucky cavalryman. Since they both knew escape across the yard was impossible, they agreed that a tunnel offered their only hope. From a third-floor window Colonel Rose had seen workmen removing the manhole covers of a sewer along a nearby street. If they dug a tunnel to that sewer, he believed, they would be able to travel along it to whatever waterway it emptied into — either a canal not far away, or the James River.

Their tunnel would have to be dug from the prison basement, and Hamilton figured out how to reach that basement from their first-floor kitchen. One night they went quietly down the stairs, after the other prisoners were asleep. They had told no one of their plan, for fear it would reach the ears of the guards. Together they moved one of their two cook stoves away from the fireplace in the kitchen wall. Next, using the only tools they had — two ordinary table knives — they scraped the soot from the lower part of the fireplace and put it carefully aside. Then they began to scrape away the mortar between the bricks. At the end of several hours, a few of the bricks had been loosened and could actually be removed.

But no more could be done that night. The prisoners upstairs would soon be waking and their own absence would be discovered. Carefully the men replaced the bricks they had removed and covered them with the soot they had saved. Then they moved the stove back into place and crept upstairs to get some rest for the next night's work.

After several more nights of hard labor in the kitchen, they asked a few trusted friends to join them. At the end of twelve nights their group of half a dozen men had made a narrow passageway down into the one basement room the guards had no reason to enter.

A cutaway view of the Libby Prison and the escape route dug by its prisoners. Redrawn from *The Story of the Famous Tunnel Escape from the Libby Prison* by Major A. G. Hamilton. *Courtesy U.S. Army Military Institute.*

They were ready to start the tunnel they hoped would lead them to freedom.

After removing enough bricks from the building's foundation wall to give them an opening about two feet square, they took turns digging into the earth outside the building. Their tools were those two knives and an old chisel they had found. The earth they dug out was hidden beneath the old bedding straw piled in one corner of the basement.

They felt little danger from the guards walking about in the prison yard, some eight feet above them. But they didn't like the squealing rats that scrambled over their legs every night.

The work went fairly smoothly at first, through earth that was easy to dig and firm enough to stand without support. But the work was tedious and uncomfortable. A man had to push himself into the tunnel head first, on his stomach. In one hand he held his candle. In the other was the shallow box into which he would put the earth he dug out. That wooden box had been one of the cuspidors into which the tobacco-chewing prisoners spit their tobacco juice. Now a strip of blanket was tied to each side of it. One strip was coiled into the box, along with the prisoner's digging tool. The other end stretched behind the box to the tunnel entrance, where another man kept hold of it.

When the box was full of earth, the digger took firm hold of the strip of blanket (which he had earlier removed from inside the box), and signaled by tugging on the other strip stretched to the entrance. The box was then dragged back to the basement, emptied, and pulled forward to the tunnel face again by the strip the digger still held.

But the longer the tunnel grew, the more time it took to drag the box back and forth, and the more foul the air became inside the tunnel. Soon a digger could work only a short time before his candle began to flicker for lack of oxygen. Then, to avoid suffocation, he had to wriggle back into the basement as quickly as possible, and wait until some fresh air had flowed into the tunnel.

For the sake of faster progress, Rose and Hamilton confided their secret to still more men, until they had three crews of five men each. Each crew worked for a definite period each night, timing its stint by the hourly calls of the patrolling guards outside.

Each man in a crew took turns at the five necessary tasks: digging, pulling back the box of earth, hiding that earth under the straw, fanning air into the tunnel by waving a hat in front of it, and standing watch in the kitchen. And each night the last work crew had to replace the bricks in the kitchen fireplace and return the stove to its daytime position, leaving no sign of what had gone on below during the hours of darkness.

The first sign of moisture at the tunnel's face raised everyone's spirits. It told them they were nearing the sewer they had been aiming for. But the moisture soon turned into serious water seepage. And the rapid increase of the seepage showed that the sewer must be above their tunnel, rather than beneath it as they had hoped. Threatened by complete flooding of the tunnel, the men did the only thing they could do: they pushed earth back into the tunnel to block the flow of water, and replaced the bricks in the foundation wall.

All those long hours of work had resulted in failure. But Rose immediately offered another plan. They would start a new tunnel in a different direction, he said. This one would be aimed at a big yard across the street from the prison. The yard was surrounded by a high board fence, but the prisoners could see down into it from their upstairs windows. The warehouse and other buildings that stood there were used by the prison guards, but were normally deserted at night. And men emerging from a tunnel there would almost certainly be invisible to the night guards on the prison side of the fence.

Spurred on by Rose's determination, the men made their second opening in the basement wall. Again the work went easily and quickly at first. Then the men found themselves up against a wall of large logs that had probably once formed part of a building's foundation. Their knives and their chisel were useless against that iron-hard barrier. Their second tunnel, too, had to be abandoned.

Thirty-eight days had now been spent on fruitless efforts to escape from Libby Prison. But Rose insisted on still a third try. This new tunnel would also be aimed at the fenced yard, but along a line that — he hoped — would avoid the obstacle of the logs. So the work began once more, with the same three-shift system, the same primitive tools, the same squealing, scurrying rats.

After a week the men measured their tunnel and tried to guess if it was long enough to have passed beneath the fence. They decided it needed several more nights' work. At the end of that time, very cautiously, they began to dig upward. Each man, in turn, scraped away at the earth above his head, pausing every few seconds to listen for some sound that would tell him he was close to the surface.

One digger, knife in hand, suddenly scraped against something hard. He felt it with his fingers. It was a stone — quite a large stone. He scraped around its edge, trying to loosen it.

Suddenly he felt it shift. He was barely able to duck aside as it fell past him and landed with a thud on the tunnel floor.

The fresh air flowing down across his face told him in an instant that the tunnel was now open to the sky. In that same instant he heard a voice.

"What was that?" a guard was asking.

"Probably a rat," another answered.

There was silence for a long moment, while the tunneler held his breath.

"I guess so," the first guard said finally, and their footsteps moved away.

The digger backed out of the tunnel as quickly as he could with his news. There was now an opening into the tunnel, and the tunnel still had not reached the fence. That opening was thus almost certain to be discovered as soon as the sun came up.

Colonel Rose took instant command. He stuffed straw into an old pair of trousers, picked up the battered remains of an old shoe, and pushing both objects before him he squeezed into the tunnel. When he arrived at the opening, and had made sure no sentries were near, he reached through and laid the old shoe near the edge of the hole. Then he covered the straw-stuffed trousers with earth, and forced them into the opening.

When he returned to the basement, he sent another man into the tunnel to wedge a board under the trousers, so that they couldn't fall down out of the hole. Now, if no one stepped directly on them, they might protect the prisoners' secret.

At the first sign of light, a few hours later, many eyes were staring down from the prison's upper windows. All the watchers agreed that the hole itself could not be noticed. But the battered shoe, half hidden by dry weeds, told them that only a couple of yards now separated the end of their tunnel from the fence under which it must pass.

Two nights later a second upward shaft was dug and the tunneler who broke through heaved a sigh of relief. He was inside the fenced area, out of sight of the prison guards. Even better than that, he had emerged beneath a small shed raised above the ground on wooden posts.

The next day was spent in feverish preparations. Each of the fifteen diggers chose a friend to escape with him. They were to leave in pairs, with a ten-minute wait between departures. Order and complete silence were necessary so that the guards would not be alerted.

But now other prisoners learned what was happening, and many of them wanted to leave through the tunnel too. A plan was finally devised to give them their chance without risking the safety of the fifteen men who had dug the tunnel and their fifteen friends. After those thirty men had left, it was agreed, an hour would elapse during which no one went near the tunnel. Then any men who wished could leave at their own pace, although all traces of the escape route must finally be covered so that it might be used again some day.

At eight o'clock on the evening of February 9, 1864, the fifteen pairs of men solemnly shook hands all around. They knew they might never see each other again. Colonel Rose entered the tunnel for the last time, with his friend. Major Hamilton was the next to enter, with his friend, and at ten-minute intervals the thirteen other pairs followed.

An hour after they had all left, other prisoners began arriving at the tunnel entrance. By dawn, one hundred and nine of them had made the fifty-foot underground journey to freedom, and the bricks had been replaced in the kitchen wall. Dozens of other men were hoping to leave the next night.

But that morning Libby Prison exploded in an uproar. Enraged prison officials started a search for the means by which so many of their prisoners had disappeared. Their search was unsuccessful. So they decided prison guards had been bribed to let the men go, and arrested all who had been on duty that night. The number of night guards in the camp was doubled.

Shortly afterwards, the tunnel was discovered, and it was filled in before anyone else could use it.

Of those one hundred and nine Union officers who had escaped, and were trying to reach their own lines, fifty-nine finally succeeded. Two men were drowned. And forty-eight were recaptured, some after many days of cold, hunger, and terrible hardship. Among those forty-eight was Colonel Rose. But along with other prisoners of war, he was released when the war ended little more than a year later. And some twenty years afterward he was finally persuaded to write an account of one of the most famous of all escape stories — the story of the Libby Prison tunnel.

Glossary

Bends — A disease that can strike anyone under high air pressure if that pressure is too quickly lowered.

Blow-out — The escape of compressed air through a tunnel wall.

Build-and-sink — A method of underwater tunnel construction by which the tunnel is built on land and then floated out and sunk in its prepared position.

Cut-and-cover — A method of building a tunnel by digging an open trench and then roofing it over.

Demoralized rock — The name used by Hoosac Tunnel miners for a muddy gravel that collapsed as fast as it was dug.

Double jacking — A method of drilling holes in rock by a three-man team: two men pounding with sledgehammers on a steel drill held by the third.

Holing-through — The moment when two teams of tunnelers, digging toward each other, break through a final barrier of rock or earth and see each other through the hole they've made.

Jumbo — A large drilling platform on which many miners can drill holes in the tunnel face at the same time.

Legging — A method by which boatmen move a canal boat through a narrow tunnel by pushing against the tunnel roof or walls with their feet.

Mechanical mole — A machine for cutting through soft rock, limestone, or shale. A mole cuts a hole as large in diameter as the finished tunnel will be.

Miners — Tunnelers who dig through rock.

Muckers — Tunnel workers who haul loose rock or muck out of a tunnel under construction.

Nipper boys — Young tunnel workers who kept double-jacking teams supplied with sharp rock drills, and took dull drills to the blacksmith shop for resharpening.

Round — A series of five different jobs that are done repeatedly while digging a tunnel through rock or earth. The five jobs are: drilling, loading drilled holes with explosives, blasting, ventilating area, and mucking or removing loosened material.

Sandhog — The American name for underwater tunnelers.

Shield — A device that encloses and protects tunnelers digging an underwater tunnel, and at the same time supports the walls and ceiling of the newly dug tunnel until they can be lined.

Shotcreting — Spraying a cement mixture on the inside of a tunnel to form a concrete lining.

Stand-up time — The length of time rock, earth, gravel, sand or other material will stand unsupported while a tunnel is being dug through it.

Tunnel face — The solid wall of rock or earth facing miners as they work.

Index